PagePlus X3
Resource Guide

This book has been created and output in entirety using Serif PagePlus.

How to contact us

Contacting Serif technical support

Our support mission is to provide fast, friendly technical advice and support from a team of on-call experts. Technical support is provided from our Web support page, and useful information can be obtained via our web-based forums (see below). There are no pricing policies after the 30 day money back guarantee period.

UK/International/
US Technical Support :   **http://www.serif.com/support**

Additional Serif contact information

Web:

Serif Web Site: **http://www.serif.com**

Forums: **http://www.serif.com/forums.asp**

Main office (UK, Europe):

The Software Centre, PO Box 2000, Nottingham, NG11 7GW, UK

Main:	(0115) 914 2000
Registration (UK only):	(0800) 376 1989
Sales (UK only):	(0800) 376 7070
Customer Service (UK/International):	**http://www.serif.com/support**
General Fax:	(0115) 914 2020

North American office (US, Canada):

The Software Center, 13 Columbia Drive, Suite 5, Amherst NH 03031, USA

Main:	(603) 889-8650
Registration:	(800) 794-6876
Sales:	(800) 55-SERIF or 557-3743
Customer Service:	**http://www.serif.com/support**
General Fax:	(603) 889-1127

International enquiries

Please contact our main office.

Introduction

Welcome to the PagePlus X3 Resource Guide! Whether you are new to PagePlus or a seasoned desktop publisher, the *Resource Guide* offers content to help you get the best out of PagePlus. From a range of novice and professional tutorials to get you started or help you accomplish a complex project, to full-colour previews of the **Design Packs** and **Logo Templates**, the *Resource Guide* is something you'll return to time and time again.

About the Resource Guide

The *Resource Guide* is your key to getting even more out of PagePlus and is organized into the following chapters:

- **Tutorials**—Illustrated, step-by-step training covering the basics of PagePlus and desktop publishing, along with some more challenging projects.

- **Design Packs**—A useful reference gallery showing page previews of the various **Design Pack** template sets available with PagePlus X3 and its **Resource DVD**.

- **Logo Templates**—Colour previews of the pre-designed logo templates included with PagePlus.

How the Resource Guide was made

This full-colour *Resource Guide* was created and output using PagePlus, and employing many PagePlus features. These features include:

- BookPlus to unify separate publications with a common page numbering system.

- Mail and Photo Merge with Repeating Areas to automatically create pages with picture content based on a folder of images.

- Find and Replace functionality to apply text styles consistently and quickly throughout the text.

Finally, the content was incorporated into a PagePlus Book comprised of multiple publication chapters. The book was then published as a press-ready PDF—accurately maintaining all text, fonts, images, and native colouring—in a CMYK colour format suitable for professional printing.

Contents

Projects

Aimed at both beginners and more experienced PagePlus users, these illustrated, step-by-step projects provide you with the opportunity to experiment with various tools and techniques.

In each project, you'll create a different type of publication from scratch. You'll improve your mastery of PagePlus tools, and pick up valuable tips and tricks along the way.

To access files needed by the projects, browse to the **...\Tutorials\Workspace** folder in your PagePlus installation directory. In a standard installation, you'll find this in the following location:

C:\Program Files\Serif\PagePlus\X3

We hope you enjoy working through these exercises!

The tutorials are presented as PDF files, which you can print out or view on screen.

If viewing on screen, you can quickly switch between PagePlus and the tutorial document by pressing the **Alt + Tab** keys.

Projects

Creating a Real Estate Flyer

PagePlus provides a wide selection of design templates, which you can use as starting points for your own publications.

In this project, we'll start with a real estate flyer template and customize it to suit our own requirements. You can use the same principles to customize any of the design templates.

In this exercise, you'll learn how to:

- Work with master pages.
- Update user details.
- Move and align objects.
- Replace, add, resize, and crop images.
- Use the Media Bar.
- Create, edit, and format text.
- Insert logos.
- Apply colour fills.
- Add pages.
- Preview and print a publication.
- Print double-sided documents.

Creating a Real Estate Flyer

This project assumes that you'll be printing your flyer on A4 or Letter sized paper, and that you are using the sample images provided in the **...\Tutorials\Workspace\Real Estate** folder. In a standard installation, you'll find this folder in the following location:

C:\Program Files\Serif\PagePlus\X3

If you prefer, you can use your own images.

1. Updating the template

The first section of this tutorial shows you how to edit and updated the existing elements of the template publication.

> 💡 If you've switched the Startup Wizard off, you can switch it back on.
>
> 1 Click **Tools > Options**.
> 2 In the **Options** dialog, on the **General** page, select the **Use startup wizard** check box.

To open the design template

1 On the **File** menu, click **New from Startup Wizard**.

2 In the Startup Wizard, click **Use Design Template**.

3 In the **Choose a Template** dialog, in the left **Templates** pane, expand the **Flyers & Posters > Flyers** subcategory.

4 Click **A4 > Portrait** or **Letter > Portrait** (depending on your product version) and view the thumbnail samples on the right.

5 Select the **Real Estate Listing** template and click **Open**.

6 If the **User Details** dialog opens, click **Cancel** to close it (we'll return to this dialog later).

This is a single page publication containing a selection of images, text objects, and shapes.

Let's start by replacing the images of the property with our own.

To replace an image

1 Click on the main image and then click the  **Replace Picture** icon.

2 In the **Import Picture** dialog, browse to your **...\Workspace\Real Estate** folder.

3 Select the **6294764.jpg** file and click **Open**.

   The photo is updated on the page and automatically scaled to fit.

4 Repeat the previous steps to replace the other photos of the house with **5321355.jpg** and **6294768.jpg**, as illustrated on the right.

Our next task is to replace the photo of the realtor.

As this image has been placed on the **master page**, we need to be in Master Page view to work with this object.

To view and update the master page

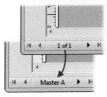

1 In the lower left corner of the workspace, click the **Current Page** box (currently showing that you are viewing page '1 of 1') to switch to Master Page view.

> 💡 Typically, a master page is used for storing elements that appear on multiple pages of a publication—a logo, background, page numbers, and so on.

In this publication, the photo of the realtor, the company information, and the decorative background elements have been placed on the master page.

2   Select the photo. Because this image has been placed inside a picture frame, additional controls display beneath it.

3   Click 🖳 **Replace Picture** and replace the photo with **1513h0004.jpg**.

4   Click 🖐 **Pan** and drag on the image to reposition it inside its frame.

> ❗ Picture frames are shaped containers similar to text frames. You can use these as placeholders, and then import or drag your pictures picture them. At any time you can swap a different picture into the same frame. This allows you to separate the container from its content, and incorporate picture frames into your layout irrespective of the actual images that will go inside them.
>
> For details, see "Adding picture frames" in online Help.

Now let's update the company information. This is taken directly from user details fields, which means that we can make all our edits in the **User Details** dialog and then update everything at once.

Jane Jones
jjones@jjones&corealty.com
www.jjones&corealty.com

To update user details

1   On the **Tools** menu, click **Set User Details**.

2   In the **User Details** dialog, on the **Business** tab, click and drag to highlight the default text and then type in your own information.

3   When you've finished, click **Update**.

    On the page, the text is updated automatically.

You can create your own custom user details fields on the **Custom** tab of the **User Details** dialog.

4   **Optional:** To insert additional user details fields, click **Insert > Information > User Details**, select the field to add and click **OK**.

As the length of your user details will probably differ from the original fields, you may need to reposition or realign some of your text objects.

To move a text object

*   Select the object and then click and drag the ✥ **Move** button that displays in the upper left corner.

- or -

*   Click to select the text object's border (the border changes colour to show that the entire object is selected), and then drag into position using the ✥ **Move** cursor.

To align objects

1   Use the ⬉ **Pointer** tool to select the objects you want to align. To do this, you can:

    *   Click and drag to draw a bounding box around the objects.

    - or -

    *   Hold down the **Shift** key and click each object in turn.

2   On the **Align** tab, click your required alignment option(s).

While we're on the master page, let's also replace the logo. We'll show you two ways to do this:

- By inserting a predesigned logo (which you can edit in LogoStudio). You might choose this method if you don't already have a company logo and want some ideas, or a starting point, for creating one.

- By inserting your own logo graphic file. Use this method if you already have a company logo and want to add it to your flyer.

To insert a LogoStudio logo

1　Select the logo graphic and then press the **Delete** key.

2　On the Tools toolbar, click **Insert Logo**.

3　In the **Insert Logo** dialog, browse the thumbnails and select the logo of your choice.

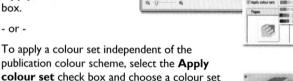

4　To apply the colour scheme of your publication to the logo, clear the **Apply colour set** check box.

- or -

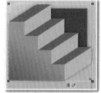

To apply a colour set independent of the publication colour scheme, select the **Apply colour set** check box and choose a colour set from the drop-down list.

5　Click **Open**.

6　To insert the logo at default size, simply click the mouse; to set the logo size, click and drag.

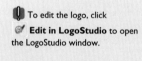

To edit the logo, click
Edit in LogoStudio to open the LogoStudio window.

To insert your own logo

1 Select the logo graphic and press the **Delete** key.

2 On the Tools toolbar, click  **Import Picture**.

3 In the **Import Picture** dialog, browse to and select your own logo graphic file and then click **Open**.

4 Click and drag on your page to set the size of the logo, then drag into position on your page.

Before returning to Normal page view, let's change the colour of the background elements.

To apply a colour fill

1 Click to select the large blue rectangle.

2 On the **Swatches** tab, click the ⬜ **Fill** button (currently showing that this object has a blue fill applied).

3 Click to expand the ▦ ▾ **Palettes** drop down list and select the palette of your choice.

4 Click a colour swatch to apply the colour fill to the selected shape.

5 Repeat the previous steps to apply colour fills to the other two shapes.

6 Click the **Current Page** box to return to Normal page view.

In Normal page view, we can see another colour fill we need to adjust.

7 Follow the previous steps to apply a complementary colour fill to the central horizontal band.

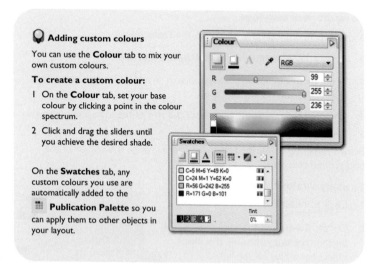

Adding custom colours

You can use the **Colour** tab to mix your own custom colours.

To create a custom colour:

1 On the **Colour** tab, set your base colour by clicking a point in the colour spectrum.

2 Click and drag the sliders until you achieve the desired shade.

On the **Swatches** tab, any custom colours you use are automatically added to the

Publication Palette so you can apply them to other objects in your layout.

Let's now turn our attention to the text objects. We need to update these with the details of our listing.

In PagePlus, you can use the ![pointer] **Pointer** tool to select, edit, and format text directly on the page,

To select and edit text

1 Click the ![pointer] **Pointer** tool and then:

   • Drag to select a range of text.

     - or -

   • Double-click to select a word.

     - or -

   • Triple-click to select a paragraph.

     The selected text area is shaded in blue for clear editing.

2 Type in your own text as required.

To apply formatting and colour to text

Select the text and then:

- To apply character and paragraph formatting, use the controls on the Text context toolbar.

- To apply colour, click 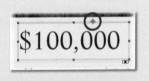 **Text** on the **Swatches** tab, and then click a colour swatch.

For quick and easy formatting and recolouring of an entire text object:

1 Select the text object by clicking on its border (the border changes colour).

2 Use the Text context toolbar and/or **Swatches** tab as described above.

When you have finished making your changes, you're ready to preview and print your flyer.

To preview a publication

1 On the Standard toolbar, click **Print Preview** to see how your flyer will appear on the printed page.

2 If you are happy with the results, click **Print**.

3 In the **Print** dialog, set your printer options and the number of copies to print, and then click **Print**.

2. Adding new content

We've updated the template objects with our own information, and these changes may well be sufficient for your needs. But now let's suppose you want to create a double-sided flyer and add more text and images.

The final section of this tutorial shows how to:

- Add new master and standard pages.
- Import, resize, and crop images.
- Create artistic and frame text.
- Print double-sided documents.

Adding pages

We'll create a new master page and assign it to a new publication page.

To create a new master page

1   At the top of the **Pages** tab, click to expand the upper **Master Pages** panel, currently displaying just the one page— **Master A**.

2   Click the 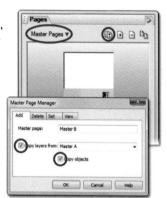 **Page Manager** button.

3   In the **Master Page Manager** dialog, click the **Add** tab.

4   Select the **Copy layers from** and **Copy objects** check boxes. Click **OK**.

5   The new master page—**Master B**—is created and opened in the workspace.

This page is an identical copy of Master A. We want to keep all the same page objects, except for the realtor photo and details.

6   Using the ![pointer] **Pointer** tool, click and drag to draw a bounding box around the photograph and its text frame.

7   Press the **Delete** key to remove these objects from the page.

Our next task is to assign the new master page to a new publication page.

To create a new standard page

1 On the **Pages** tab, in the lower Pages panel, click the 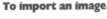 **Page Manager** button.

2 In the **Page Manager** dialog, click the **Insert** tab.

3 In the **Master page** drop-down list, select **Master B**. Click **OK**.

The new page is added to the publication and opened in the workspace.

Working with images

You can add images by importing them directly onto the page, or you can use the **Media Bar** to temporarily store your images before placing them.

To import an image

1 On the Tools toolbar, click Import Picture.

2 In the **Import Picture** dialog, browse to and select an image (to select multiple images, hold down the **Ctrl** key and then click each image in turn).

3 Click **Open**.

4 Click on your page to place each image at the default size, or click and drag to set the size of each image.

To add images to the Media Bar

1 At the bottom of the workspace, click the ——— handle to display the **Media Bar**.

2 On the **Media Bar**, in the rightmost drop-down list, select **Temporary Album**.

3 Click Add Image.

4 In the **Open** dialog, browse to the ...**Workspace\Real Estate** folder.

5 Press and hold down the **Ctrl** key and select the **6294750.jpg** and **6294792.jpg** files. Click **Open**.

The images display as thumbnails in the **Media Bar**.

> 💡 You can also drag an image file from any Windows folder directly onto the **Media Bar**.

6 To place an image, drag its thumbnail from the **Media Bar** onto the page.

Images that have been added to the publication are marked with a green checkmark.

By default, images are added to a temporary album, but you can create more permanent albums from which you can retrieve stored images at any time.

To create a named album

1 Click New Album .

2 In the **New Album** dialog, type a name for the album, and then click Add Image or Add Folder.

3 In the **Open** dialog, navigate to and select an image file, or the folder containing your images.

4 Choose whether images are to be embedded or linked.

5 Click **Open** to add the list of images to the dialog.

6 Click **OK**.

Once placed on the page, you may need to resize or crop your imported images.

To resize an image

1 Select the image.

2 Click one of the corner selection handles and drag to a new position.

To crop an image

1 Select the image.

2 On the Attributes toolbar, on the Crop flyout, click the ⬚ **Square Crop** tool.

3 Click and drag an edge or corner handle towards the centre of the image.

4 **Optional:** To apply a feathered edge to the crop outline, use the **Feather** drop-down menu on the Crop context toolbar.

Adding text

PagePlus lets you create both **artistic text** and standard and shaped **text frames**.

- **Artistic text** is generally used for standalone text with special effects. When you resize an artistic text object, the text resizes accordingly.

- **Text frames** work equally well for single words, standalone paragraphs, or multi page articles. Text inside a text frame remains the same size when you resize the frame.

To create artistic text

1 On the Text flyout, click the **Λ Artistic Text** tool.

2 To create text at the default size, click on the page and start typing.

- or -

To set the size of the text, click and drag with the cross-hair cursor to set the desired text size, and then start typing.

Setting text properties

- To set artistic or frame text properties before typing: Use the controls on the Text context toolbar.

- To set text colour before typing: On the **Swatches** or **Colour** tab, click the A **Text** button, and then click a colour.

To create a text frame

1 On the Tools toolbar, on the Text Frames flyout, click the ⬚ **Standard Text Frame** tool (for a standard rectangular frame), or choose one of the **Shaped Frame** tools.

2 To create a new frame at a default size, click on the page.

- or -

To set the size of the frame, click and drag.

3 To add text, simply start typing.

4 If required, click and drag to adjust the dimensions of the frame.

When you're happy with page 2 of your flyer, you're ready to print.

Printing double-sided documents

If your printer supports duplex (two-sided) printing, you can automatically print out your publication as a double-sided document by setting the double-sided printing options in the PagePlus **Print** dialog.

If your printer does not support duplex printing, you can use the **Manual Duplex Printing** wizard to configure your standard printer to print on both sides of your paper.

To print on a printer that supports duplex printing

1 On the Standard toolbar, click  **Print**.

2 In the **Print** dialog, on the **General** tab, select an option from the **Double-sided options** drop-down list:

- To print on both sides, flipping on the short side of the paper, select **Automatic Duplex, flip short side**.

- To print on both sides, flipping on the long side of the paper, select **Automatic Duplex**.

3 Click **Print**.

To set up your printer for manual duplex printing

1 On the **File** menu, click **Setup Manual Duplex Printing**.

2 A list of printers available for manual duplex printing is displayed. Select the printer that you wish to configure and click **Next**.

3 Follow the instructions, selecting the options that apply to your printout, and clicking **Next** when you are ready to proceed to the next step.

4 **Optional:** At the end of the configuration, you can choose to print out the instructions for manual duplex printing with this printer in the future.

If you would like to do this, click **Yes**.

5 Click **Finish**.

The optional printout can potentially save time and money by helping to prevent you from loading the paper incorrectly.

If you decide later that you don't want the instruction page, you can turn it off by running through the Setup dialogs again.

To print using manual duplex printing

1   On the Standard toolbar, click 🖨 **Print**.

2   In the **Print** dialog, set your printing options, and in the **Double-sided options** drop-down list, choose **Manual Duplex**.

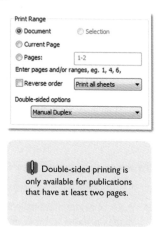

3   Click **Print**.

4   The first set of pages will print, along with an instruction page (if you requested one).

5   Place the paper back in the tray and press **Continue** to print the other side.

> Double-sided printing is only available for publications that have at least two pages.

6   You should now have a double-sided printout!

In this tutorial, we've introduced you to the basic tools and techniques required to create and customize the key components of a PagePlus document—pages, text, and images.

Of course, PagePlus provides numerous other features, but the topics we've covered here should be sufficient for many of your desktop publishing projects.

Creating a Photo Scrapbook

Every scrapbook is unique. Some are specifically for school events, others for vacations, while many simply record memories of children growing up and of family celebrations. Whatever memories they record, scrapbooks provide an ideal way for you to display and show your favourite photographs.

In this project, we'll show you how to combine photos with text and graphics to create a photo scrapbook. We've provided sample photographs, but you can use your own if you prefer.

In this exercise, you'll learn how to:

- Create a multi-page document.
- Work with master pages.
- Create QuickShapes.
- Work with colour, transparency, filter effects, and fills.
- Import, position, resize, and crop images.
- Create and apply object styles.
- Work with frame and artistic text.
- Wrap text to image borders.
- Adjust image colour, brightness, and contrast.

Creating a Photo Scrapbook

In this exercise, you'll create a photo scrapbook, which you can print on a home printer. Our sample images were taken on a family holiday in Scotland, so you'll notice a Scottish theme to the layout. You can use your own images and theme if you prefer. Your photographs don't have to be perfect—we'll show you how to crop them and make various adjustments later. If you don't have photos to hand, you'll find some samples to work with in your **...\Tutorials\Workspace\Scrapbook** folder—in a standard installation, you'll find this in the following location:

C:\Program Files\Serif\PagePlus\X3

Let's begin by creating and saving a blank document. We'll then create a cover page and show you how to apply a background design using a master page.

To create and save a new publication

1   In PagePlus, click **File**, point to **New**, click **New from Startup Wizard**, and then click **Start New Publication**.

2   In the dialog, click **Regular/Normal** and then click **Portrait**. Click the **A4** or **Letter** template and click **Open**.

3   To save the new document, click **File > Save**. Save the file as **Scrapbook.ppp**.

First, we'll design an attractive cover for the scrapbook using a stylized version of the St. Andrew's Cross as a background. We'll create this part of the layout on a master page.

> 💡 Try to avoid importing very large image files. Even if these are scaled down on the publication page, the original file size is preserved. As a rule, downscale your images using photo-editing software (such as PhotoPlus), then import them into PagePlus.

> 💡 **Master pages** are part of the structure of your publication, and provide a flexible way to store background elements that you'd like to appear on more than one page—for example a logo, background, header/footer, or border design.

To create a master page

1 On the **View** menu, click **Master Page**. The master page view opens and 'Master A' is now displayed.

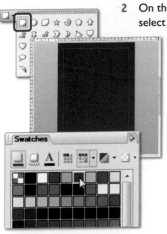

2 On the Tools toolbar, on the QuickShape flyout, select the **Quick Rectangle**.

3 Click and drag to create a rectangle to cover the entire page. It doesn't matter if you go over the edges of the page as these will not be printed.

4 With the rectangle selected, on the right of the workspace, click the **Swatches** tab.

5 On the ⬛ **Palette** drop-down list, select the **Standard RGB** palette, and then click the blue swatch. Click on the 🔲 **Line** button and then click the 🔲 **None** swatch. This will remove the outer line.

This solid blue rectangle will form the background of our St. Andrew's Cross, which will sit behind text and photos on our cover page. Rather than being solid, we want to give it a more transparent appearance.

6 With the rectangle still selected, click the **Transparency** tab, click the **Gradient** button, and then click the **Linear Transparency 40** swatch. (Hover the cursor over the swatches to view their labels.)

We've applied a blue to white transparency gradient. We'll now use the **Line** tool to create the white cross to complete our flag.

7 On the Tools toolbar, on the Line flyout, click the ✒ **Pen** tool.

8 Draw a diagonal line across the page—click once at the top left corner of the page to start the line, hold down the mouse button, drag to the lower right corner, and then release the mouse button.

9 Click the **Pointer** tool, then click on the line and drag it to create a curve, as illustrated.

10 With the line selected, click the **Line** tab (or click **Format > Line and Border**), and increase the line weight to 64 pt.

11 Click the **Swatches** tab, click the **Line** button, and then click the white swatch. You should now have a heavy white line.

12 Right-click the line, and then click **Filter Effects**.

13 In the **Filter Effects** dialog, select the **Feather** check box, and increase the blur to 12 pt. Click **OK**.

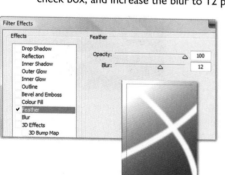

14 Repeat steps 7 to 13 to create and format a second line, as illustrated.

We've finished the flag design so let's now assign it to the cover page—page 1 of our publication. With our master page safely in place, we'll then be able to add and manipulate other PagePlus objects without disturbing our carefully created background elements.

To assign a master page

1   On the Hintline toolbar, click the
    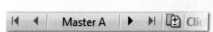 **Page Manager** button to open
    the **Page Manager** dialog. Click the
    Set tab.

2   In the **Publication page(s)** drop-
    down list, select 'Page 1.'

3   In the **Uses master page** list, select
    'Master A.'

4   Click **OK**, and then switch back to normal page view by clicking **View**,
    then **Normal** (or by clicking Master A at the lower left of the Hintline
    toolbar).

Next, we'll import images and add an interesting 'polaroid' effect using the
Filter Effects dialog and the **Line** studio tab. We'll also use standard text
frames to create a title.

To import and position an image

1   On the Tools toolbar, click 🖼 **Import Picture**. In the **Import
    Picture** dialog, browse to locate the photograph you want to open, or
    browse to the ...**Workspace\Scrapbook** folder and open
    123_2338.jpg.

2   When the cursor changes to a ⊹🖼 click on the page to insert the
    image. Note that the Picture tools are
    displayed in the Picture context
    toolbar.

3   Resize the image—click one of its
    corner handles and drag it to a new
    position. You'll want this image to be
    about 6 cm by 4 cm.

4   On the Tools toolbar,
    from the Selection
    flyout, click the
    ↻ **Rotate** tool.

> 💡 When working with
> multiple images, instead of
> importing them one at a
> time, why not add them all to
> the **Media Bar**? As you
> work on your document, you
> can then quickly view your
> images and drag and drop
> them onto the page when
> you need them. You'll find
> more details in the **How To**
> tab and in online Help.

5 Select the photograph, hover over one of its handles (the **Pointer** changes to the **Rotate** cursor), click and drag to rotate the shape.

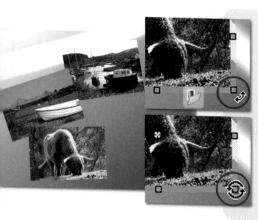

In PagePlus there are two types of rotation available: **Pointer** tool rotation and the **Rotate** tool.

To rotate an object using the **Pointer** tool, select the object, hover the cursor just outside one of the handles. Click and drag to rotate.

More advanced options are available with the **Rotate** tool, such as changing the ⟡ rotation origin. For more information, online Help.

6 Hover over the object until the pointer changes to the ✛ **Move** cursor. Click and drag the image into position.

7 Repeat steps 1 to 6 to import and position additional images as required.

The images look okay, but we can create more impact and visual interest by adding some creative effects. In these next steps, you'll see how adding a line and a drop shadow can really make a difference by giving the impression of depth. Although we're applying this effect to a photograph, you can use the same procedure to apply lines, borders, and filter effects to many other PagePlus objects—shapes, artistic text, and so on.

To add a line to an object

1 Select the object. On the **Line** tab, set the line weight to 5 pt (with either the slider or the drop down menu) and set the style to a single, solid line.

2 To change the line colour, on the **Swatches** tab, click the 🔲 **Line** button and then click the white colour swatch to apply it.

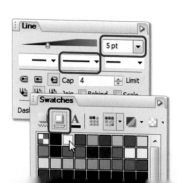

To add a drop shadow to an object

1   With the object still selected, on the Attributes toolbar, click
    fx **Filter Effects**.

2   In the **Filter Effects**
    dialog:

    • From the **Effects** list,
      click the **Drop Shadow**
      check box.

    • Set the **Opacity** to 50.

    • Set the **Blur** and the
      Distance to 6 pt.

    • Set the **Angle** to 135.

    • To see a preview of the
      effect, expand the dialog
      by clicking the
      ▷ **Show/Hide**
      preview button.

    • Click **OK**.

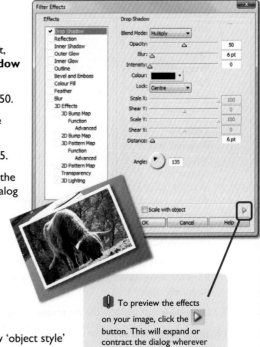

You can now save this new 'object style'
and apply it to other objects in your
publication.

🔋 To preview the effects
on your image, click the ▷
button. This will expand or
contract the dialog wherever
you see it.

💡 **Object styles** benefit your design efforts in much the same way as text styles
and colour schemes. Once you've created a set of attributes that you like—properties
like line colour, fill, border, and so on—you can save this cluster of attributes as a
named style. PagePlus remembers which objects are using that style, and the style
appears on the **Styles** tab.

To create and save an object style

1 Right-click the object, choose **Format > Object Style > Create**.

2 In the **Style Attributes Editor**, in the lower right **Style Properties** section, type a name for the new style.

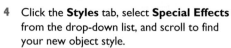

3 Click the **Browse** button and select a category in which to save the style (we've chosen **Special Effects**). Click **OK**. Click **OK** once more to close the **Style Attributes Editor**.

4 Click the **Styles** tab, select **Special Effects** from the drop-down list, and scroll to find your new object style.

5 Let's apply our style to the other two photographs.

To apply an object style to one or more objects

1 With the object(s) selected, click the **Styles** tab.

2 Select the style category from the drop-down list, and then click the style thumbnail to apply it to the object(s).

All we need now is a title and our cover page is complete.

It's often tempting to use large bold fonts for titles. When laying out a publication, however, try to keep the whole composition in mind. In this case, we don't want to detract from the background design and photos so we'll keep it simple.

To create and format a title

1   On the Tools toolbar, click the  **Standard Text Frame** tool, then click and drag to insert a frame to the right of the photos.

2   In the text frame, type "Scotland 2005" and then click and drag to select the text (or press **Ctrl+A**).

3   On the Text context toolbar, choose the font size and style for your heading. We've used a 36 pt, Celtic style of font.

4   With the text frame selected, resize it to fit the text—click one of the frame handles, hold down the left mouse button, and then drag to the new position.

5   In the text frame, double-click the word 'Scotland' to select it.

6   On the **Swatches** tab, click the ▲ **Text** button and then click a white swatch.

7   Repeat step 6 to change the colour of '2005' to blue.

8   Finally, repeat steps 1 to 6 to create a second text frame containing the words "holiday memories..." This time, we used the same font as before and changed the size to 20 pt and the font colour to white.

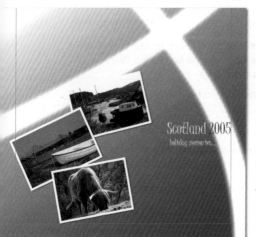

For the inside pages of our scrapbook, we'll use some of the features we've already worked with—master pages, text frames, object styles, and so on—but we'll also introduce you to some other features. We'll first create a watermark effect, which we'll use as a background for our scrapbook. To do this, we'll apply a gradient fill and colour to an imported image.

To create a watermark design on a master page

1   Click the **Pages** tab, click the arrow to expand the **Master Pages** pane, and then click the ⊞ **Add** button. A blank page opens and 'Master B' is now displayed at the lower left of the Hintline toolbar.

2   On the Tools toolbar, click 🖾 **Import Picture**.

3   In the **Import Picture** dialog, browse to the ...**Workspace\\Scrapbook** folder and open the **Thistle.jpg** file.

4   When the cursor changes to a ✛🖾 click on the page to insert the image.

5   Resize the image so that the head of the thistle is approximately 6 cm high, and then move the whole image to the lower right of the page.

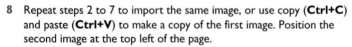

6   With the image selected, click the **Transparency** tab, click the ◼ **Gradient** button, and then click the **Ellipse Transparency 70** swatch.

7   Click the **Swatches** tab, click the ◢ **Fill** button, and then click a light grey swatch. We used RGB (187, 187, 187).

8   Repeat steps 2 to 7 to import the same image, or use copy (**Ctrl+C**) and paste (**Ctrl+V**) to make a copy of the first image. Position the second image at the top left of the page.

Let's assign this master page (Master B) to the second page of our scrapbook.

To assign a master page

1   On the **Pages** tab, in the **Pages** pane, click ⊞ **Add** to add a second standard page.

2   On the Hintline toolbar, click the ⊞ **Page Manager** button.

3 In the **Page Manager** dialog, click the **Set** tab.

   • In the **Publication page(s)** drop-down list, select 'Page 2.'

   • In the **Uses master page** list, select 'Master B.' Click **OK**.

4 Switch back to normal page view by clicking Master B at the lower left of the Hintline toolbar, or by selecting **Normal** from the **View** menu.

In this next section, you'll import some photographs and add titles and captions using standard and artistic text frames. We'll show you how to improve a photograph by adjusting brightness and contrast settings, and how to change a colour photograph into a dramatic black and white image.

You should now have 'page 2 of 2' open in the workspace. The page should be blank except for the watermark background. Let's begin by importing the four images we want to display on this page. As you've already imported and applied an object style to the images for the cover page, we'll summarize the following steps. However, return to the previous sections if you feel you need to follow the more detailed step-by-step procedures.

To import and position images and apply an object style

1 On the Tools toolbar, click 🖼 **Import Picture**.

2 In the **Import Picture** dialog, browse to the locate the image you want to open, or choose one from your **Workspace** folder.

3 Repeat steps 1 and 2 to import additional images, resizing and positioning them as required.

4 Select all of the images (click on one, press and hold the **Shift** key, and then click each of the others in turn), click the **Styles** tab, and then apply your custom object style.

We're now ready to add some text objects to the page. Let's first create a title using artistic text.

To create a title using artistic text

1   On the Tools toolbar, click the **A** **Artistic Text** tool, click in the top left corner, and then type your title.

2   Click in the line of text and press **Ctrl+A** to select everything.

3   On the Text context toolbar, choose the font style for your heading. We used clean style, 30 pt font.

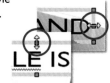

4   With the text frame still selected, click one of the frame handles and then drag the title until it overlaps the edge of the photograph at the top of the page.

Click the upper centre frame handle to enlarge the height of the text.

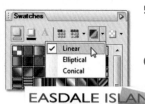

5   On the **Swatches** tab, click the **Gradient** button, and then select **Linear** from the drop-down list.

6   Select the **Linear Fill 186** swatch.

Now let's add a caption for this first photo. We'll use a standard text frame, change the font style and colour, and set text-wrapping options.

To create and format a photo caption

1   On the Tools toolbar, click the **Standard Text Frame** tool, then click and drag to insert a frame under the title and to the left of the first photo.

2   In the text frame, type your photo caption and then click and drag to select the text (or press **Ctrl+A**).

3   On the Text context toolbar, choose the font size and style for your heading. Here we used a 14 pt, handwriting style font. Resize the text frame to fit the text.

4   Click **Format**, and then click **Character**. In the **Text Style** dialog, under **Character**, click **Font**. Click the **Text colour** drop-down palette and select a dark grey colour swatch.

5   Click and drag the text frame to the right, so that it overlaps the edge of the photo.

We want our caption to 'wrap' to the contours of the photograph. We can easily do this by changing the wrap settings for the photograph.

> 💡 You can wrap frame text around an artistic text object, a table or another frame, or even flow text inside a graphic. For more information, see online Help.

To wrap text around an object

1   Select the photograph and click the 🔲 **Wrap Settings** button on the toolbar (or right-click the photo and choose **Wrap Settings**).

2   In the **Wrap Settings** dialog, do the following:

    • In the **Wrapping** section, click **Tight**.

    • In the **Wrap To** section, click **Left**.

    • In the **Distance from text** section, enter a value of '0.20 cm' in each of the four boxes.

    • Click **OK**.

3   Repeat the previous steps to add captions for each of the other three photos, wrapping the text where necessary.

Wrap Settings

Wrapping

None | Top & bottom | Square | Tight | Inside | Edge

Wrap To

All | Both sides | Left | Right | Largest side

Distance from text

Left: 0.2 cm   Top: 0.2 cm
Right: 0.2 cm   Bottom: 0.2 cm

☐ Crop object to wrap outline   OK   Cancel   Help

Time to move on to the final page of this scrapbook.

We'll now show you how to get the best out of your photos using some exciting PagePlus features.

You'll be familiar with many of the following procedures, so we'll just summarize them and let you go back to the previous sections if you need to.

To lay out the final page

1 Click the 🔲 **Page Manager** button, click the **Set** tab, and assign **Master B** to Page 3 of your publication.

2 Click the 🖼 **Import Picture** button and import five more images of your choice.

Note that in the next section we'll be working with a photograph of Barcaldine Castle. If you want to work with the same image, you'll find it in the **...\Workspace\Scrapbook** folder.

3 Click the **Styles** tab and apply your custom photo edge object style to each photograph.

4 Add captions using either the 🔲 ▾ **Standard Text Frame** or **A** ▾ **Artistic Text** tool.

5 Add special effects if you wish.

🔋 For the words 'Out and About,' we used artistic text and applied **Linear Fill 32** from the **Swatches** tab.

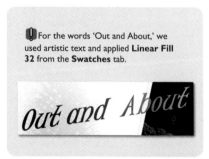

Let's make some adjustments to two of our photographs. To begin, we'll take the image of the Black Castle and convert it to black and white. You can use your own photo if you prefer.

To convert an image to black and white

1 Click the image to select it, and then click the **Swatches** tab.

2 On the **Swatches** tab, click the  **Fill** button, and then click the black swatch in the upper left of the swatches panel.

> 💡 To give your photos an 'aged' effect: On the Picture context toolbar, click **Recolour Picture**, and select a dark brown swatch, for example RGB (138, 90, 48). Instant sepia tone!

Now for our final task. PagePlus provides a host of features to allow you to perform common photo corrections such as adjusting contrast, modifying shadows and highlights, even fixing red eye. We'll use the options on the Picture context toolbar to adjust brightness and contrast.

To adjust image brightness and contrast

1 Select the image and the Picture context toolbar displays.

2 To adjust the brightness click:

- ◎ to increase brightness.

- ◎ to decrease brightness.

3 To adjust contrast click:

- ◎ to increase contrast.

- ◎ to decrease contrast.

> 💡 To let PagePlus automatically manage the image adjustments for you use the ◎ **Auto Level** and ◎ **Auto Contrast** buttons.

We'll now crop some of the background from our Black Knight photo. You can practise this technique on any of your photos. (For more on cropping techniques, see the "Creative Cropping" tutorial.)

To crop an image

1 With the image selected, on the Attributes toolbar, click the ☐ **Square Crop** tool.

2 Click one of the handles on the edge of the image (the cursor changes to the **Square Crop** cursor) and drag towards the centre until you have achieved the desired effect.

3 If required, repeat the process to crop away any other unwanted areas of the image.

Q To fine-tune your cropped image:

Click in the image (the cursor changes to 🖑), and then drag to reposition the image inside the crop boundary. To restore the cropped object to its original shape: Click **Remove Crop** on the Crop flyout.

That's it—you've created the cover and the first two pages of your first photo scrapbook. We hope you've enjoyed the process and have learned a few PagePlus tricks along the way.

When creating scrapbooks and photo albums in the future, several options are open to you:

• Use this scrapbook layout as a template and import your own photos—simply right-click an existing photo, click **Replace Picture**, and then choose your new photo. Don't forget to change the captions too!

Q Use QuickShapes and transparency to 'sticky tape' your photos to the page—for step-by-step instructions, see the "Creating a Sales Flyer" tutorial.

- or -

• Start with a photo album design template and add your own images and captions.

To do this, click **File**, point to **New**, click **New from Startup Wizard**, and then click **Use Design Template**. In the **Choose a Template** dialog, expand the **Photo Albums** category. You're sure to find something to suit your taste.

Whichever option you choose, we're sure you'll enjoy creating beautiful scrapbooks and photo albums to hold those special memories and share with friends and family.

Creating a Business Card

Learn all about logos, branding, and identity as we show you the secrets of effective logo and business card design.

PagePlus tools give you the flexibility to lay out text and graphic objects, and design logos for your business cards—and it's easy to set up your printer to print multiple copies on one sheet. Creating your own design also allows you to make modifications on the fly, and then preview and print out your results before choosing a final layout. We'll show you how to:

- Set up page and printer options.
- Use artistic text and graphics objects to design a logo.
- Use a variety of typefaces to create different effects.
- Use colour effectively in a layout.
- Position and align text and graphics objects.
- Group related objects together.
- Lay out a small publication.

Creating a Business Card

You may have noticed that some business cards look better than others. Why is this? Is it the layout, the colours, the typeface, or a combination of all of these elements? Great designs are not a mystery and you don't need professional graphic design skills to produce a business card. By following some simple rules, you can ensure that your business cards look professional and convey the right image.

In this exercise, we'll create a logo and design a business card for a fictitious recruitment company. We'll demonstrate five different logo designs and explain how the elements in each of them work together to convey a different image. To begin, let's create our publication and set up page and printer options.

To set up a business card publication

1   Open PagePlus, click **File**, point to **New**, click **New from Startup Wizard**, and then click **Start New Publication**.

2   In the dialog, click **Small Publications**, and then click **Business Cards**. Click the **Wide Business Card** template, and then click **Open**.

3   On the **File** menu, click **Page Setup**, then click **Create Custom** to open the **Small Publication Setup** dialog.

- The left preview pane shows how the business cards will be laid out at print time.

- In the **Size** section, the default **Width** (8.50 cm) and **Height** (5.50 cm) of a 'wide business card' document are displayed.

- The **Gap X** and **Gap Y** values denote the size of the spaces that will be left between the business cards when they are laid out side-by-side on one sheet of paper.

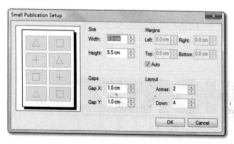

- In the **Margins** section, clear the **Auto** box to set your own page margin size, or leave it selected to use the PagePlus default settings.

- The **Layout** section tells you how many business cards will fit across and down a single page, using the current margin and gap settings.

Let's remove the gap between the business cards so that we won't have to cut out each card individually after we have printed them.

4   Set both the **Gap X** and **Gap Y** values to '0.' In the preview pane, you'll notice that the layout changes to reflect the new settings. Note also that we can now fit ten cards to a page, rather than eight.

5   Click **OK** to return to the **Page Setup** dialog. Click the **Print Setup** button.

6   In the **Print Setup** dialog, click the **Properties** button.

The dialog that opens is printer-specific—the settings depend on the printer you're using.

The **Orientation** setting is generally available regardless of the printer and lets you choose whether to print your page in **Portrait** or **Landscape** style.

> When printing small publications such as business cards, try changing the orientation and then checking back in the **Page Setup** dialog to see which orientation will fit more copies on a single page.

7   Click **OK** three times to close the printer, **Print Setup**, and **Page Setup** dialogs.

We've set up our business card publication. We're going to work on our logo design next, so we don't need the business card document at the moment. Let's save it and keep it open as we'll need to come back to it later.

- On the **File** menu, click **Save**. Save the document as **Business Card.ppp**.

- Follow the steps outlined previously to create a new blank document. This time select a **Regular/Normal** 'Portrait' size document.

You'll use this new document to experiment with your logo design. Once you've settled on a final layout, you can then copy it on to your business card.

> A **logo** is a unique name, symbol, or trademark of a company or organization. Well-designed logos provide brand name recognition and promote a business presence. They achieve this because people process an image in their mind more easily than words. In addition, visual stimulation produces a more effective and long-lasting impact on the audience's memory than words alone.

In the following section, we'll show you the different techniques we used to create our five sample logos. We'll discuss the effectiveness of each, and give you some design tips to help you create your own.

Example 1

In our first example, we used a modern font in two different sizes and colours.

We expanded the text spacing and incorporated 'sunrise-coloured' graphic bars to give the impression of horizontal width—playing on the word 'horizon.' Let's break this down so you can see exactly how the effect was achieved.

H O R I Z O N | R E C R U I T M E N T

To create and format artistic text

1   On the Tools toolbar, click the **A Artistic Text** tool.

2   Click anywhere in the document and type

'HORIZON 1 RECRUITMENT.'   **HORIZON 1 RECRUITMENT**
Note that we've typed a letter "1"
between the two words, leaving a space on either side.

3   Click in the line of text and press **Ctrl+A** to select both words.

4   Use the Text context toolbar, or the   **HORIZON 1 RECRUITMENT**
Fonts tab, to choose the font style
for your text.

5   In the text frame, double-   **HORIZON | RECRUITMENT**
click the word
'HORIZON' to highlight it,
then on the **Character** tab, change the **T Font size** to 18 pt.

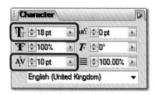

6   Repeat step 5 to change the size of the letter 'I' to 24 pt, and the size of the word 'RECRUITMENT' to 12.5 pt.

7   Click in the line of text and press **Ctrl+A** to select both words.

8   On the **Character** tab, change the **A̮V̮ Spacing** to a value of 10 pt.

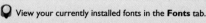

View your currently installed fonts in the **Fonts** tab.

Hover over a listed font for an in-place preview of your selected text—if you like what you see, simply click to apply the font.

By making these minor adjustments to font size and spacing, we have already created the impression of horizontal width and given a much more modern look and feel to the line of text.

H O R I Z O N | R E C R U I T M E N T

Let's change the text colour of the word 'RECRUITMENT.' This is a quick and easy way to create visual interest and contrast in a layout.

To change font colour

1 In the text frame, click and drag to highlight the letter 'I' and word 'RECRUITMENT.'

2 On the **Swatches** tab, click the **Text colour** and choose a palette from the **Palette** flyout.

3 Select a dark blue-grey swatch and click to apply the colour.

C=88 M=56 Y=0 K=0

H O R I Z O N | R E C R U I T M E N T

Design Tip

Contrast is an important consideration when designing any publication layout. The simplest and most obvious contrast is black text on a white background, but you can be more adventurous and use opposite colours on the colour wheel—such colour pairs (e.g. red and green, blue and orange) are actually termed 'contrasting colours.' You'll find information to help you choose the right colours for your publication in the "Working With Colour Schemes" tutorial.

Now to introduce a graphic element to our design. In the following section, we'll show you how to create the coloured bars using a basic Quick Shape. You'll be working at quite a detailed level, so it's a good idea to zoom in at this point.

To zoom into a publication

- On the **View** toolbar, click  **Zoom In**.

  - or -

- Click the **Zoom** tool, and then drag out a rectangular bounding box on the page to define a region to zoom in to. The zoom percentage adjusts accordingly, fitting the designated region into the window.

  To zoom out, hold down the **Shift** key when dragging. Double-click the button to display the page at actual size (100%).

To create and format a Quick Shape

1 Click the **Quick Shape** button on the Tools toolbar and select the **Quick Rectangle** from the flyout.

2 Click and drag to create a rectangle under the first two letters of 'HORIZON.'

3 Select the rectangle, then on the **Swatches** tab, click the **Palette** drop-down list and select the **Standard RGB** palette.

4 Click the **Fill** button and select the pink (RGB 255, 95, 255) swatch.

5 With the rectangle still selected, click the **Line** button and select **None** or .

Now that we've created the template for our shape, we can copy and paste it to quickly create another three identical shapes.

To copy and paste an object

1   Select the object, right-click, and then click **Copy**.

2   Right-click again and click **Paste**.

3   Repeat steps 1 and 2 to create four identical shapes. PagePlus pastes the copies one on top of the other.

4   Click on each of the copies in turn and position them so that they span the word 'HORIZON.' Don't worry about spacing them exactly—we can use PagePlus alignment tools to do this.

To align objects on a page

1   Press and hold down the **Shift** key, then use the ↖ **Pointer** tool to click on each of the four bars. A blue bounding box appears around the group of objects.

2   On the **Align** tab click ⬆ **Top** and ⬌ **Space Evenly Across**. If necessary, clear the **Include margins** check box.

The bars are now perfectly spaced and aligned. Let's go ahead and change their colours.

To change the colour of an object

1   Click to select the object—in this case the second bar on the left.

2   Click the **Swatches** tab, click the ⬛ **Fill** button, and then click one of the pale green colour swatches. We used RGB (188, 252, 184).

3   Repeat steps 1 and 2 to colour the other two bars. We used RGB (256, 136, 32)—orange, and RGB (0, 132, 132)—dark green.

H O R I Z O N | R E C R U I T M E N T

Congratulations, you've just created a simple, but effective company logo. As you can see, it doesn't require complicated procedures, or professional design skills. In fact, the simplest designs often work the best.

To further demonstrate this point, we'll show you a few more examples, all of which use simple techniques that you can adapt to suit your own needs.

Example 2

In this example, we used a fluid modern font (with slightly expanded text spacing) for the main company name 'Horizon,' contrasting it with a simpler font for the word 'Recruitment.' Playful loose fonts like this are often used for holiday agency companies.

We also created a colourful sun motif over the 'o.'

To do this, we used three capital 'I' letters, colouring, rotating, and resizing each of them individually. You could achieve the same effect with a simple Quick Tear (convert the shape to curves—you'll find this command on the **Tools** menu—and then edit the shape as required.)

Example 3

This example builds on the previous themes and ideas. Here, the focus is on the sunrise over the letter 'i'. This logo has a more 'technical' look and feel, more appropriate for an I.T. job agency for example.

A clean and simple font was used, with the shade of each letter deepening towards the centre of the word. With this design, the letter 'i' and its sunrise motif could be used as a separate branding identity for the company.

Example 4

This example takes a very different direction. The heavy bold typeface (Arial Black) represents strength, while the colours were introduced to soften the company image. The letter spacing of the word 'RECRUITMENT' was expanded.

A simple, but effective technique—basic coloured Quick Shapes were used to add colour behind the letters.

While this logo has quite a generic look and feel, it would be very recognizable.

Example 5

Here, we've created a **typographic letterform** logo formed by placing the letters 'h' and 'r' one on top of the other. Again, we've used Quick Shapes for the coloured graphic bars.

Typographic letterform logos are preferred usually because of their effective means towards trademark development. This logo doesn't share the same themes as the previous examples (horizons, sunrises)—it's quite generic. It does, however, have strong distinctiveness, **retention, modularity,** and **equity**.

Now that you have created your logo, why don't you add it to the **My Designs** category in the **Gallery** tab? To do this, **Ctrl**-drag a copy of the logo onto the tab. This will ensure that it is available to use throughout your PagePlus publications, just like any other gallery object.

If you need more logo ideas, take a look at the prebuilt, fully customizable logos in LogoStudio. For more information, see online Help and the **How To** tab.

Modularity: Describes how well a logo can be used across multiple applications (different printed media for example). In particular, how a typographic letterform logo can be used in conjunction with its more traditional full title logo (in our example, 'Horizon Recruitment').

Retention: Used to describe the process of a viewer's first interaction with the logo. If a symbol is too easy to read and figure out, the viewer feels no sense of discovery—no personal investment or connection with the logo. Having to digest the logo and work it out (in this case from the letters h + r within the letterform) ensures the logo stays with them in the subconscious.

Equity: Refers to a logo's 'staying power' without the need to redesign. It is desirable to be modern and trendy—but not so much so that the logo may go out of fashion. It's generally better, therefore, to develop a more timeless identity.

Having covered how to design a company logo, we can now look at identity—how a company presents itself on printed media. Our focus will be the business card.

Creating a Business Card

For this exercise we'll use the typographic letterform logo we created in Example 5.

A business card should be laid out in a way that is balanced. Different areas saying different things and presenting different information, all in order of appropriateness.

In our sample card for Horizon Recruitment, it's appropriate that the company logo is the focal point. The aim of this business card is to promote the company, while providing a means of direct contact with the person who gives away the card.

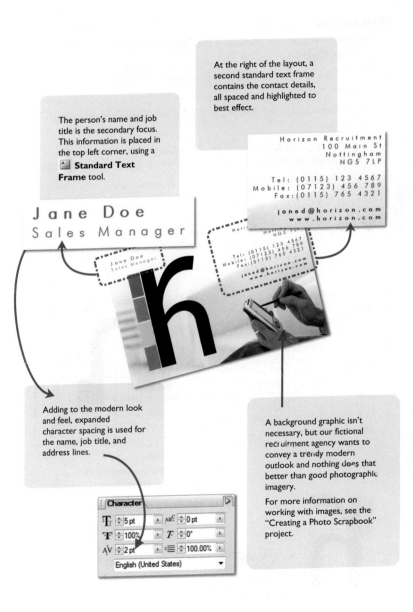

At the right of the layout, a second standard text frame contains the contact details, all spaced and highlighted to best effect.

The person's name and job title is the secondary focus. This information is placed in the top left corner, using a **Standard Text Frame** tool.

Horizon Recruitment
100 Main St
Nottingham
NG5 7LP

Tel: (0115) 123 4567
Mobile: (07123) 456 789
Fax: (0115) 765 4321

janed@horizon.com
www.horizon.com

Jane Doe
Sales Manager

Adding to the modern look and feel, expanded character spacing is used for the name, job title, and address lines.

A background graphic isn't necessary, but our fictional recruitment agency wants to convey a trendy modern outlook and nothing does that better than good photographic imagery.

For more information on working with images, see the "Creating a Photo Scrapbook" project.

To lay out a business card

1 Select your entire logo design and then on the **Edit** menu, click **Copy** (or press **Ctrl+C**).

2 Now return to your business card document by selecting it from the **Window** menu.

3 On the **Edit** menu, click **Paste** (or press **Ctrl+V**) to paste your logo into the document.

4 With the logo selected, resize it by clicking one of the frame handles, holding down the left mouse button, and then dragging to the new size.

5 Drag the resized logo into position on the business card.

> When you paste or import a new image, or select an existing one, note that the **Picture** tools display in the context toolbar.

6 On the Tools toolbar, click the 🖼 **Standard Text Frame** tool, then click and drag to insert a frame in the top left corner.

7 In the text frame, type your name, press **Enter**, and then type your job title.

8 In the text frame, click and drag to select the text (or press **Ctrl+A**).

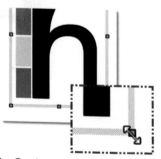

9 On the Text context toolbar, choose the font size and style for your heading, adjust the letter spacing if necessary.

10 Repeat steps 6 to 9 to add a second text frame to the right of the logo. Type in the company name and address, and your contact details.

Although a background graphic isn't necessary (and may sometimes be inappropriate), in our example, it certainly adds visual appeal and interest.

It's easy to do this—simply click the  **Import Picture** button and choose your image. Once you have the image in place, select it, and then on the toolbar, click the **Send to Back** button to place it behind all the other objects on the page.

> You can also add a background graphic to a master page. For more information on master pages, see the "Creating a Photo Scrapbook" project, or refer to the PagePlus online Help.

Well done! In these few pages, you've learned how to design an effective business logo and use it in a business card layout.

In this example we have clearly conveyed a fast-moving, modern, and powerful corporate image. But this is just the beginning. A well-designed logo can be used for many different purposes—business stationery, brochures, newsletters, and so on. We hope we've given you an insight into logo and business card design and inspired you to create a logo that will work for your company to promote a distinct and recognizable identity.

Creating a Newsletter

The goal of good newsletter design is to entice the target audience to read the information it contains. You can do this through your choice of layout style, nameplate, typefaces, and images—all of which should reflect the content.

In this project, you'll create a four-page newsletter from scratch. You'll learn how to:

- Create a multi-page document.
- Create master pages.
- Work with artistic text.
- Lay out standard and shaped text frames and flow text between frames.
- Work with grouped elements.
- Create and format a QuickShape.
- Import, position, resize, and crop images.
- Create and apply object styles.
- Wrap text around objects and fit text to a curve.

Creating a Newsletter

In the following exercise, we'll create a newsletter for a kids' Karate Club. We'll explain how to lay out a newsletter publication, providing design tips along the way. We'll also show you some examples of good and bad newsletter design. Use your own images, or our sample images—located in your PagePlus installation directory

(usually **C:\Program Files\Serif\PagePlus\X3**),

in the **...\Tutorials\Workspace\Newsletter** folder.

To begin, let's create our newsletter publication and set up the pages.

To create and set up a newsletter publication

1 Click **File**, point to **New**, click **New from Startup Wizard**, and then click **Start New Publication**.

2 In the dialog, click **Regular/Normal**, and then click **Portrait**. Click the **A4** or **Letter** template, and click **Open**.

3 At the lower left of the workspace, on the Hintline toolbar, click the 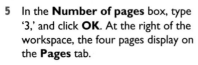 **Page Manager** button.

4 In the **Page Manager** dialog, click the **Insert** tab.

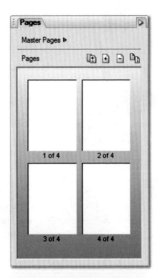

5 In the **Number of pages** box, type '3,' and click **OK**. At the right of the workspace, the four pages display on the **Pages** tab.

6 On the **File** menu, click **Page Setup**.

The **Page Setup** dialog allows you to modify the publication dimensions and format. We're going to keep all the default settings except one.

7 At the lower left of the dialog, click to select the **Facing pages** check box. (Note that the **Dual master pages** box is automatically selected by default.) Click **OK**.

You'll notice now that pages 2 and 3 display together, as facing pages. This page setup is particularly useful when laying out multi-page publications because it allows you to see your pages exactly as they will be viewed in the document.

8 To save the document, click **File** then **Save**. Save the file as **Newsletter.ppp**.

> 🔵 **Page size** and **orientation** settings are fundamental to your layout, and are defined when a new publication is first created. You can adjust these aspects of a publication at any time—as a rule, however, make changes before you've gone too far with your layout. In practice, your working limit is likely to be set by the capabilities of your desktop printer.

Our next job is to set up the **master pages**—pages that are shared by the entire publication. You can use master pages for objects such as watermarks or background designs that you want to appear on multiple pages of a publication (see the "Creating a Photo Scrapbook" project). We're going to use master pages to set up the page numbering of our newsletter.

To insert page numbers on a master page

1 On the **Pages** tab, expand the **Master Pages** category and double-click the 'Master A' page. The master page view opens and 'Master A' is now displayed in the Hintline toolbar at the lower left of the workspace.

2 On the Tools toolbar, click the 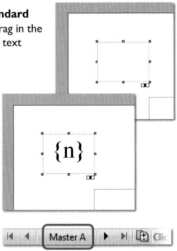 **Standard Text Frame** tool, and then click and drag in the upper left corner of the page to insert a text frame.

3 Click in the text frame, then on the **Insert** menu, click **Page Number**.

4 With the text frame still selected, on the Text context toolbar, click **Align Centre**.

5 Repeat steps 2 to 4 to insert a page number in the upper right corner of the facing page.

6 Return to the main publication pages by clicking Master A on the Hintline toolbar at the lower left of the workspace or by double-clicking page 1 on the **Pages** tab.

7 In the lower left corner of the workspace, on the Hintline toolbar, click the **View previous page** and **View next page** arrows. You'll see that the page number now appears on all four pages of the document.

As a general rule, the first page of a newsletter is not numbered. To remove the number from our front page, we'll simply assign the master pages to all pages except page 1.

To assign a master page

1 To the left of the Hintline toolbar, click the **Page Manager** button, and then click the **Set** tab.

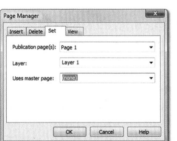

2 In the **Page Manager** dialog:

- In the **Publication page(s)** drop-down list, select 'Page 1.'

- In the **Uses master page** list, select '(none).'

3 Click **OK**.

4 Go to the first page to confirm that the page number is no longer displayed.

We've laid the groundwork for our newsletter publication and can now start to work on the layout. We'll begin on page 1, with the nameplate.

To create a nameplate using artistic text

1 On the Tools toolbar, click the A **Artistic Text** tool.

2 Click in the document and type "karatecamp."

3 Select the text frame by clicking on its border—the frame will turn dark grey.

> The banner on the front of a newsletter that identifies the publication is its **nameplate**. The nameplate usually contains the name of the newsletter, possibly graphics or a logo, and perhaps a subtitle, motto, and publication information such as volume and issue number or date.

4 Use the **Fonts** tab to find a font that preferably has both a heavy and a light style. Click the heavy style to apply it to the text. Set the text size to 90 pt using the Text context toolbar.

5 In the text frame, click and drag to highlight just the word 'camp,' then use the **Fonts** tab to change the font to the light version.

karatecamp

6 Insert a second artistic text frame containing the word 'Newsletter', in the same heavy font but with a size of 30 pt.

7 Select the border of the text object and use the **Character** tab to make the text "Expanded" by a value of 10 pt.

karatecamp
Newsletter

8 Position this second text frame below the first one, as illustrated.

By making these simple adjustments to font style, size, and spacing, we have created contrast—an important element in any type of publication layout.

We've created our newsletter nameplate out of two separate artistic text elements, which we've positioned carefully. We can now turn these two objects into a group object. We'll then be able to position, resize, or rotate them all at the same time—this is a useful feature to use when designing nameplates or logos that you might want to use repeatedly, across different types of printed media.

> The **Fonts** tab allows you to preview a font before you apply it. Select your text, then hover over a listed font for an in-place preview —if you like what you see, simply click to apply the font to your text.
>
> The tab also hosts a **quick search** feature to filter fonts by name, attribute, or type.

To create a group from a multiple selection

1   Select the first object, press and hold the **Shift** key, and then select the next object.

    - or -

    Use the ⬧ **Pointer** tool to draw a selection bounding box around both objects.

2   Click the ⬚ **Group** button below the selection.

    - or -

    On the **Arrange** menu, choose **Group Objects**.

> To turn a group back into a multiple selection
>
> • Click the ⬚ **Ungroup** button below the selection.
>
> - or -
>
> • Choose **Ungroup Objects** from the **Arrange** menu.

Let's add an image to the front page of our newsletter. When selecting an image for the first page of a newsletter, choose something that will grab the attention of your audience. Make sure, however, that it is also representative of the content of your publication.

To import an image

1   Click outside the text frame group to deselect it. On the Tools
    toolbar, click the ▨ **Import Picture** button.

2   In the **Import Picture** dialog, browse to the
    ...**Workspace\\Newsletter** folder and open the **15745851.png** file.

3   Click the **Embed picture** and **Place at Native dpi** options, and
    then click **Open**.

4   When the cursor changes to a ⁺▪, click in your page and drag to
    insert the image. Note that the Picture tools are displayed in the
    context toolbar.

Embedded images
become part of the
publication file, while linking
places a reference copy of
the image on the page and
preserves a connection to
the original file. Each
approach has its pros and
cons (for more information,
see online Help).

We're going to give this image more impact by adding a border effect. In PagePlus, a border is a repeating, decorative element that can be set to enclose an object. Borders work especially well with imported pictures.

To add a border to an image

1 Select the image, then click the **Line** tab.

2 On the **Line** tab:

- In the line weight box, click the drop-down arrow and select a weight of 7.5 pt.

- In the line style box, click the drop-down arrow and select a dashed line.

- Adjust the **Dash Pattern** slider as illustrated.

Notice that we've left a space to the left of our image. We're going to fill this space with a **standard text frame** containing the address and contact details.

To create and format text

1 On the Tools toolbar, click the ▣ **Standard Text Frame** tool, then click and drag to insert a frame to the left of the photograph.

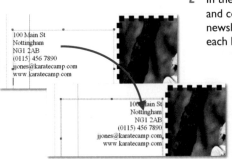

2 In the text frame, type the address and contact details for the newsletter, pressing **Enter** between each line.

3 With the text frame selected, on the Text context toolbar:

- Click the ☰ **Align Right** button.

- Choose a plain font and set it to approximately 10 pt.

2005 Annual Camp Review

4   Repeat the previous steps to add a caption for the photo.

💡 Keep it simple by using a single typeface or typeface family. Introduce contrast by adjusting size, style, letter spacing, colour, etc. Or use bold, italic, and light and condensed versions of the same family. Play with alignment and text leading. You can create very different effects simply by changing the amount of white space surrounding the text.

In the following section, we'll create and format a QuickShape, which we'll then convert to a shaped text frame. We'll use this frame for our first piece of body text.

To create a QuickShape and convert it to a shaped frame

1   On the Tools toolbar, on the QuickShapes flyout, select the ▱ **Quick Button**.

2   Keeping inside the blue page margins (if you can't see the margins, click **View > Guidelines**), click and drag to create a shape that extends the width of the page, and from the 17 cm mark on the vertical ruler, down to the bottom of the page.

When the shape is selected you'll notice small white boxes—control handles—on each side. You can alter the shape by dragging these handles.

3   On the left side of the shape, click the handle and drag it down to the bottom of the shape. Then, drag the top handle across to the right.

You're aiming to achieve the shape illustrated.

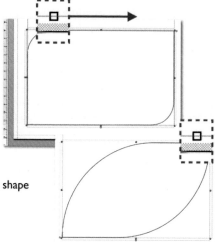

4   With the shape selected, on the **Swatches** tab:

- Click the ⬜ **Fill** button, and select a colour for your new shape (we used RGB— 208, 252, 92—from the **Standard RGB** palette).

- In the lower right corner of the tab, adjust the **Tint** to 50%.

- Click the ⬜ **Line** button, and select the same colour and tint you used for your fill.

5   To convert the shape to a text frame, start typing whilst the object is selected. You can now fill it with placeholder text. Right-click and select **Fill with Placeholder Text**.

We've created visual interest using filter effects to add a drop shadow to our text frame.

To apply a drop shadow

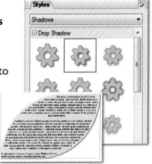

1   Select the text frame, then on the **Styles** tab, select the **Shadows** category.

2   Select the **Drop Shadow** sub-category, and then click a drop shadow thumbnail to apply the effect to the text frame.

We now need to add a caption for this text box. For this, we'll make use of another PagePlus tool that allows us to fit a line of text to a shape or line. First, we need to create the caption and a shape to fit it to.

To fit artistic text to a shape

1   Create a new QuickShape, exactly the same as the first one but slightly bigger. (This time, don't add colour.) Right-click the shape and select **Convert to Curves**.

2 With the new shape selected, on the Arrange toolbar, click the
Send to Back button. Position the shape behind the original
shaped text frame.

3 Follow the steps outlined previously
to create an artistic text object
containing the title for your text
column. We used a 30 pt heavy font.
Position the text object as illustrated.

4 Select the artistic text object and the
new shape (do not select the original
shaped text frame), then on the
Tools menu, choose **Fit Text to
Curve**. The text now flows along the
specified path and the original shape object
disappears.

You'll notice that the text is not quite in the
position we want. We can edit its path using
the **Pointer** tool.

5 Select the text path object and zoom in. You'll notice that text paths
have several unique 'handles' not found on other objects. Hover over
them and you'll see that the cursor changes for each.

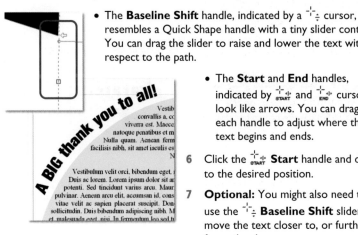

- The **Baseline Shift** handle, indicated by a ⁺ᵢ⁻₌ cursor,
  resembles a Quick Shape handle with a tiny slider control.
  You can drag the slider to raise and lower the text with
  respect to the path.

  - The **Start** and **End** handles,
    indicated by ⁺ᵢₜ and ⁺ᵢ⁻ cursors,
    look like arrows. You can drag
    each handle to adjust where the
    text begins and ends.

6 Click the ⁺ᵢₜ **Start** handle and drag
to the desired position.

7 **Optional:** You might also need to
use the ⁺ᵢ⁻₌ **Baseline Shift** slider to
move the text closer to, or further
from, the shape.

Our front page is starting to come together, but it still looks a little bare. Let's liven it up by adding another photograph and a background graphic.

1   Repeat the steps outlined previously to import the **24275544.jpg** graphic file.

2   Position the image in the lower right corner of the page.

3   With the image selected, on the Arrange toolbar, click the ⬚ **Send to Back** button to place it behind the shaped text frame.

This image adds to the depth of the layout and sets the scene—even though it's not in full view.

> 🔍 When working with multiple images, instead of importing them one at a time, why not add them all to the **Media Bar**. As you work on your document, you can then quickly view your images and drag and drop them onto the page when you need them. You'll find more details in the **How To** tab and in online Help.

Now for the final touch. We'll create a background image using another QuickShape.

To create a background graphic

1   On the Tools toolbar, on the **QuickShape** flyout, select the ⬭ **Quick Button**.

2   Keeping inside the page margins, click and drag to create a shape to fill the entire page. As you did previously, drag the handle on the left down to the bottom of the shape, and then drag the top handle across to the right.

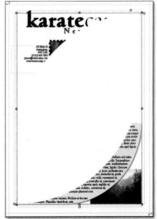

3 With the shape selected, on the
Swatches tab:

- Click the  **Fill** button, and select a
  colour for your new shape. We used
  the same colour we used
  previously—RGB (208, 252, 92).

- In the tab's lower right corner,
  change the **Tint** to 65%.

- Click the **Line** button, and select
  the same colour and tint you used
  for your fill.

- With the image selected, click
  Send to Back to place it behind
  the everything else on the page.

Congratulations! The first page of your newsletter is complete!

Let's now move on to the inside pages. Here, we're going to use a layout
that is often used in newsletter publications—multiple columns. We'll set
up our pages so that the body text flows through three columns.

To set up a multiple column frame layout

1 On the Tools toolbar, click the **Standard Text Frame** tool.

2 On page 2 of the publication, click the upper left corner of the page
margin and drag to the lower right corner to create a text frame that
completely fills the page.

3 With the frame selected, click the
Format menu, and then click **Frame
Setup**.

4 In the **Frame Setup** dialog:

- In the **Number of columns** box,
  enter a value of 3.

- In the **Gutter** box, enter a value of
  0.30 cm.

- Select the **Wrap Text Around
  Objects** check box.

- Click **OK**.

5 Insert an identical frame on page 3 by copying and pasting the frame you just created (or repeat steps 1 to 4).

At the moment, these two text frames are independent elements. However, we want to set them up so that text will flow between them.

When selected, a text frame includes a **Link** button at the lower right which allows you to import text files or control how the frame's story flows to following frames. The icon inside each frame's **Link** button denotes the state of the frame and its story text.

You can drag the column guides or use the **Frame Setup** dialog to adjust the top and bottom column blinds and the left and right column margins.

• **No Overflow**—The frame is not linked to a following frame (it's either a standalone frame or the last frame in a sequence). The end of the story text is visible.

• **Overflow**—The frame is not linked (either standalone or last frame) and there is additional story text in the overflow area. An **AutoFlow** button displays to the left of the **Link** button.

• **Continued**—The frame is linked to a following frame. The end of the story text may be visible, or it may flow into the following frame. (Note: The button icon will be red if the final frame of the sequence is overflowing, or green if there's no overflow.)

To flow text between text frames

1 Right-click the text frame on page 2 and select **Fill with Placeholder Text**. Notice the **Link** button indicating that there is no overflow.

2 Click anywhere in the text and press the **Enter** key a couple of times so that the last few lines of text no longer fit on the page.

> t Morbi tincidunt neque ut lacus.
> 2 Duis vulputate cursus orci. Mauris justo lorem, scelerisque sit amet,

The **Link** button now indicates a text overflow.

3 Click the right ▭ **Overflow** button, the cursor changes to a .

4 Now move the cursor over to the frame on page 3, and then click in the text frame when the cursor changes to a ⬙.

> 🔋 The text in a frame is called a **story:**
>
> • When you move a text frame, its story text moves with it.
>
> • When you resize a text frame, its story text flows to the new dimensions.

The missing lines of text now appear at the top of page 3's text frame. Notice too that the **Link** button on page 2's frame has changed to ▭⬇ to indicate that there is no hidden overflow and that the text continues into another frame.

If you wish, you can add more placeholder text to the story in the frames. Or you can add your own text in any of the following ways:

> 💡 Using placeholder text lets you concentrate on the visual arrangement of text frames without having to worry about their content.

- **WritePlus story editor:** Right-click on a frame and choose **Edit Story** (or select the text and press **Ctrl+E**) to start WritePlus.

- **Importing text:** Right-click on a frame and choose **Text File** to import a text file.

- **Typing into the frame:** Select the ⬉ **Pointer** tool, then click for an insertion point to type text straight into a frame, or edit existing text.

- **Pasting via the Clipboard:** Select the ⬉ **Pointer** tool and click for an insertion point in the text, then press **Ctrl+V**, or click **Edit > Paste Special** for a choice of formatting options.

- **Dragging and dropping:** Select text (e.g. in a word processor file), then drag it onto the PagePlus page.

For more detailed information on these options, see online Help.

With our basic text column layout in place, we can now place our remaining images and create captions. In the following steps, we'll import four images and set their wrap settings so that the text story flows around them.

To wrap text around an object

1 Click outside the text frames to make sure that nothing on the page is selected, then click the  **Import Picture** button and open the **7690421.jpg** file.

2 Place this image in the upper right corner of page 2 so that it covers the right column and half of the centre column.

3 Right-click the image and choose **Wrap Settings** (you can also click the ▦ **Wrap Settings** button on the **Arrange** toolbar, or click **Arrange > Wrap Settings**).

4 In the **Wrap Settings** dialog:

- In the **Wrapping** section, click **Tight**.

- In the **Wrap To** section, click **Left**.

- In the **Distance from text** section, enter '0.20 cm' in each of the four boxes.

- Click **OK**.

Your text now flows neatly around the image.

Now we'll add a caption.

5 Click the ▦ **Standard Text Frame** tool and insert a text frame below the lower right corner of the image.

6 Type your caption and format it appropriately. We used 8 pt Times New Roman. Right-click the text frame and choose **Wrap Settings**.

> PagePlus lets you wrap frame text around the contours of a separate object. Usually, this means wrapping text to a picture that overlaps or sits above a text frame. However, you can wrap frame text around an artistic text object, a table or another frame, or even flow text inside a graphic (a circle, for example).
>
> To wrap text, simply change the wrap setting for the object to which you want the text to wrap.

7 In the **Wrap Settings** dialog:

- In the **Wrapping** section, click **Square**.

- In the **Wrap To** section, click **Left**.

- In the **Distance from text** section, enter '0.20 cm' in each of the four boxes. Click **OK**.

8 Repeat the previous steps to import the **7232572.jpg** file, approximately half way down on the left-hand side of the page. This time apply a **Tight**, **Right** wrap setting.

- Add an appropriate caption and apply a **Square**, **All** wrap setting.

Now all we need is a title to finish this page. Again, we'll use a standard text frame for this.

To add a title

1 On the Tools toolbar, click the ⬚ **Standard Text Frame** tool and insert a text frame in the upper left corner of the page.

2 Size the frame so that it is slightly smaller than the column.

3 Type your title text, pressing the Enter key after each entry so that each appears on a new line. You can copy our titles, below, or use your own.

4 Select the text and on the Text context toolbar:

- Apply a 24 pt heavy typeface.

- Click the ☰ **Align Right** button.

5 If necessary, resize the frame to fit the text.

6 Right click the text frame and click **Wrap Settings**. Apply a **Tight**, **Right** wrap setting, with '0.20 cm' distance from text on all sides.

7 Finally, select the main three-column text frame and drag the centre top handle down so that the text begins halfway down the photo.

Well done, you've completed the second page of your newsletter—and you've now been introduced to all the PagePlus features you need to finish the publication.

We'll explain how we created the final pages, summarizing the steps required. We'll let you go back to the previous sections if you need to.

To create page 3

1   On page 3, the second of our three-column pages, we imported two photographs—**7689511.jpg** and **15745776.jpg**.

2   We applied wrap settings to the images and added captions.

3   To the second image we applied the same border effect used for the cover photo.

4   The third column of this page contains a testimonial letter.

We distinguished this from the rest of the text by applying an italic font style:

- Select the text and on the Text context toolbar, click the
  I **Italic** button.

5   Finally, we added the same background graphic used on page 1.

💡 You could also create a background graphic on a **master page** and then use the **Page Manager** dialog to apply it to multiple pages in your publication.

For more information on working with master pages and background effects, see the "Creating a Photo Scrapbook" project and online Help.

To create page 4

1 We copied the background graphic onto page 4, and then converted it to a shaped frame (click **Tools > Convert to Shaped Frame**).

2 We added a drop shadow effect to the shaped frame, applying the settings used on our cover page.

3 We used two different font sizes for the text in this frame.

4 We added two images— **15745722.jpg** and **2425644.jpg**, applying wrap settings to both and our border effect to the first.

5 Finally, we created text frames for a large caption (a heavy, 52 pt font), and contact details. We applied a **Tight, Right** wrap to the large caption frame.

Well done! Your newsletter is complete and you've worked with various tools and techniques to create an attractive layout. Let's now take a few moments to look at an example that doesn't work quite as well as ours. In doing so, you might be able to avoid some of the more common pitfalls that can occur when designing this type of publication.

In this example, while some advanced techniques have been used—such as the shaped text frame and text on a path, the overall composition misses the mark for the following reasons:

* The colours used are gaudy and not pleasing to the eye.

* The height spacing of the title needs adjusting, and the font used is not very imaginative.

* The white body text is hard to read against the bright green background.

- The image is not positioned well and would benefit from a border or frame.

- The overall look and feel of the layout does not convey the right image for the newsletter content, and would not appeal to the target audience.

You've reached the end of this project. We hope you've enjoyed creating the newsletter and have learned a few design tips along the way.

If you're interested in creating another type of multi-page publication, try the "Creating a Photo Scrapbook" project. If you enjoyed creating the masthead for this newsletter and want to try your hand at logo design, see "Creating a Business Card."

Whatever you choose, you should now be more familiar with PagePlus's powerful desktop publishing features—features you'll put to good use in any type of publication.

Creating a Greetings Card

Whether it's to celebrate a birthday, an anniversary, or a graduation, or simply to tell a friend you are thinking of them, we all enjoy sending and receiving greetings cards. With PagePlus, you can impress family and friends and make that special event even more memorable by making your own greetings card from scratch.

In this project, you'll learn how to:

- Lay out a folded publication.
- Use minimal colour palettes to create clean, contemporary designs.
- Work with a variety of images to create very different effects.
- Create and format text.
- Adjust image colour.
- Add transparency and reflection effects.
- Align objects on a page.
- Select the right paper for your greetings card.
- Print a greetings card.

happy birthday

Creating a Greetings Card

In this project, we'll create four different greetings card designs, which you can print on a home printer. We've supplied sample images for you to use; you'll find them in the **...\Tutorials\Workspace\Greeting Card** folder of your PagePlus installation directory

(usually **C:\Program Files\Serif\PagePlus\X3**).

We'll start by creating and saving a blank document.

To create and save a greetings card document

1 In PagePlus, click **File**, point to **New**, click **New from Startup Wizard**, and then click **Start New Publication**.

2 In the dialog, click **Folded**, and then click **Greeting Cards**. Click the first template—**Card**—and then click **Open**.

3 To save the new document, click **File**, then **Save**.

   Now to import the image for our greetings card.

To import and position an image

1 On the Tools toolbar, click
   ⬛ ▾ **Import Picture**.

2 In the **Import Picture** dialog, browse to the
   ...\Workspace\Greeting Card folder and open the **Flower.jpg** file.

3 When the cursor changes to a ⁺⬛
   click on the page to insert the image. (Note that the Picture tools are displayed in the context toolbar.)

> 🔍 Before importing into PagePlus, an image of a detailed flower was opened in PhotoPlus. The background was then removed to produce a clean and contemporary design.
>
> The same effect can also be produced using PagePlus' Image Cutout Studio. For more information, see online Help or the **How To** tab.

4 Resize the image by clicking one of its corner handles and dragging it to a new position. Make this image about 6 cm by 6 cm.

   Let's add the title. We want it to match the look and feel of the image, so we'll use a modern font style.

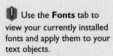 Use the **Fonts** tab to view your currently installed fonts and apply them to your text objects.

Select your text, then hover over a listed font for an in-place preview—simply click to apply the font to your text.

The tab also hosts a **quick search** feature to filter fonts by name, attribute, or type.

To create a title using artistic text

1 On the Tools toolbar, click the **A Artistic Text** tool, click about 2 cm below the image and type "happy birthday."

2 Click in the text and press **Ctrl+A** to select both words. On the Text context toolbar, choose the font style for your heading. We used Arial 18 pt.

3 With the text frame selected, click the **Character** tab at the lower right of the workspace.

4 Expand the character spacing to 10.0 pt.

To do this either, click the 'up' arrow, or click the 'right' arrow and then drag the slider.

Let's position our image and title so that they are centred horizontally on the page. PagePlus offers us a precise method of aligning objects on a page using the **Align** tab.

To align objects on a page

1 Press and hold down the **Shift** key, then use the **Pointer** tool to click on the image and the text object. A blue bounding box appears around both objects.

2 On the **Align** tab:

• Select the **Include margins** check box.

• Click **Centre Horizontally.**

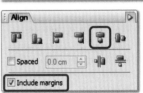

For a quick and easy effect, we'll bold and change the colour of the first letters of the title words, we'll then add a subtle reflection.

To change font colour

1 In the text frame, click and drag to select the letter 'h.'

2 On the **Swatches** tab, choose the **Standard RGB** palette from the **Palette** flyout.

3 Click the **A Text** button and choose one of the pink swatches (we used RGB (255, 127, 255).

4 With the letter still selected, click the **B Bold** button on the Text context toolbar.

5 Select the letter 'b' and repeat steps 2 to 4.

h a p p y   b i r t h d a y

Now to add a reflection. This effect looks impressive, but it's very simple to achieve. We're applying the reflection to an artistic text object; however, this effect works equally well on shapes, images, and other PagePlus objects.

To add a reflection effect to an object

1 Select the object, right-click, and then click **Copy**. Right-click again and click **Paste**.

2 Click the text object copy, then on the **Arrange** menu, click **Flip Vertical** (or right-click, select **Flip/Rotate**, and then click **Flip Vertical**).

h a p p y   b i r t h d a y
ʎ ɐ b ʌ   b ı ɹ ʇ ɥ ɒ ʎ

3 Now click the new object and move it underneath the original.

4 Click in the text object and press **Ctrl+A** to select the whole line of text.

5 On the **Swatches** tab, click the **A Text** button, and select the pink colour swatch you used previously.

h a p p y   b i r t h d a y
ʎ ɐ b ʌ   b ı ɹ ʇ ɥ ɒ ʎ

6   With both words still selected, click
    the **Transparency** tab, click the
    Solid button, and then click the
    Solid Transparency 80% swatch.

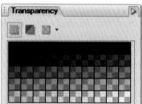

You've created the layout for your first
greetings card! As you can see, it doesn't
require complicated procedures, or
professional graphic design skills. In fact,
the simplest designs often work the best.

To further demonstrate this point, we'll
show you a few more examples, all of
which use simple techniques that you can
adapt to suit your own needs. You'll find
the sample images in your
...\Workspace\Greeting Card folder.

⚲ Try to avoid importing very large image files. Even if these are scaled down on the
publication page, the original file size is preserved. As a rule, downscale your images
first using photo-editing software (such as PhotoPlus), then import them into PagePlus.

For this party invitation, the main photo was
taken at an interesting angle, giving the
composition some depth.

Again, a minimal palette of colours was used,
the colours of the image being reproduced in
the title. We used the same technique
described above to create the reflection
effect.

For this textured abstract design, we started with an image of a vibrant textile. We cropped the photograph to show the detail of the fabric texture (you could do this with photo-editing software, or in PagePlus itself), and then placed it in the centre of the composition.

The colours of the text were then matched to the textile. To do this, we used the ✐ **Colour Picker** on the **Colour** tab.

For details, see the "Working With Colour Schemes" tutorial.

This example shows how you can turn an everyday photo of a pet or family member into a fun greetings card.

We imported our photo and then altered its colour properties by using the **Swatches** tab and the image adjustment buttons on the Picture context toolbar.

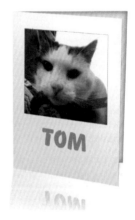

To recolour an image

1   With the image selected, click the
    ⬚ **Fill** button on the **Swatches** tab.
    Choose a colour from the palette—
    generally darker colours work best
    for this technique (for example,
    brown will create a sepia effect).

2   Use the brightness (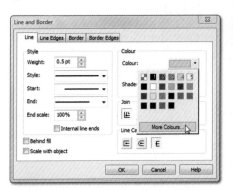 increase and decrease) and contrast
    (increase and decrease) buttons from the Picture context
    toolbar to adjust image levels.

To give the piece a more finished feel, we also added a thin border to the
image.

To add a line to an image

1   Right-click the image, click **Format**, and then click **Line and Border**.

2   In the **Line and Border** dialog:

- In the **Weight** drop-
  down list, select 0.5 pt.

- In the **Style** drop-down
  list, select 'Solid.'

- In the **Colour** section,
  select a suitable colour
  swatch (choose **more
  colours** if you need
  more choice). Click **OK**.

For the finishing touch we added a caption.
A big, bold, fun font is used to good effect
here.

When you are happy with your card layout, you can type a special
greetings in the inside pages—even a verse if you're feeling really creative!
When that's done, you're ready to print
out your card.

You can buy packs of pre-folded greetings
card paper and envelopes from most
office suppliers. Usually, this paper is
specifically intended to be used with ink
jet home printers, and comes in 160 gsm
weight.

It's worth experimenting
with printing your cards on
everyday paper first, to get
everything (margins,
positioning etc.) set up
correctly.

When you select or define a **Folded Publication** (as we did at the beginning of this exercise), PagePlus automatically performs imposition of folded publications. The settings ensure that two or four pages of the publication are printed on each sheet of paper. This saves you from having to calculate how to position and collate pairs of pages on a single larger page.

That's all there is to it! We've shown you four different examples of greetings cards to start you off, and hopefully inspire you to create your own unique designs. As you can see, all it takes is a little time and imagination.

To produce professional-looking, double-sided sheets, why not take advantage of PagePlus's duplex printing feature? It enables you to achieve great double-sided printing results, even if you don't have a printer capable of automatic duplex printing. See the section **Manual Duplex Printing** in online Help for more information.

Creating a PDF Form

Portable Document Format (PDF) form creation is one of many exciting features included in PagePlus.

You can use PDF forms for many purposes (order forms, subscription forms, billing forms, employee personal data forms, and so on) and to collect many different kinds of data.

In this project, you'll create and publish a business expense claim form, which can then be accessed by your users, filled out online, and printed.

In this exercise, you'll learn how to:

- Design a layout for a functional form.
- Create and format text objects.
- Create, resize, and position form fields.
- Set form field properties.
- Work with grouped objects.
- Replicate form fields.
- Work with ruler guides and alignment tools to position objects.
- Create a calculated form field.
- Create a custom validation script.
- Specify tabbing order of form fields.
- Publish a PDF form.

Creating a PDF Form

Let's assume that you want to create an employee expense claim form to be posted on company intranet. Employees will access the form from their own computers, fill in their expense details online, and then print out the form for processing.

Before you begin to lay out your form in PagePlus, there are couple of things you should do. Use a blank piece of paper to complete these initial steps.

First, you need to determine exactly what information you want to collect. Next, map out your design on paper. Decide on form size and structure (single or multi-page), and be sure to include graphics, text, and any other static objects.

Gathering the data

Let's think about the information we need to collect in order to process an expense claim. We'll need to know at least who is submitting the expense form, and what expenses they are claiming for. Let's assume then that we want to capture the following data:

Employee Information	Expense Information	Other Information
Employee name	Date	Reimbursement method—cheque or direct deposit
Employee number	Description—e.g. sales conference hotel bill	Whether or not a receipt is attached
Employee department	Category—travel, meals, etc.	Total expenses amount
	Amount	Employee's signature date
		Manager's signature date

Mapping out the form design

The next step is to map out the form design with paper and pencil. It's tempting to skip this and just go ahead and start dropping form objects into PagePlus. However, if you sketch your form layout on paper first, you'll end up with a better-designed form. You'll also save yourself the time and effort of having to recreate your form multiple times in PagePlus—it's unlikely that you'll be happy with your first attempt.

When drafting out your form, keep usability and visual appeal in mind. The following guidelines will help you:

- Keep your form simple and uncluttered.

- Group related form fields together.

- Give your form fields clear, meaningful labels and position them consistently relative to the object.

> If users must complete certain information on the form, be sure to indicate that these fields are mandatory. For example, with an asterisk or colour-coding.

- Provide clear and simple instructions (use ToolTips too) to help users complete the form as easily as possible.

- If you will be collecting data via hardcopy printout, avoid unnecessary or complex graphics that will use up ink and take too long to print.

- Be careful when using colour on your forms. While useful for emphasizing and enhancing certain sections of your form, too much colour can be distracting. Again, if your form will be printed out, you should use colour sparingly.

We drafted out the form design illustrated here, which we'll show you how to reproduce in PagePlus. You can use our design, or one of your own if you prefer.

Let's get started...

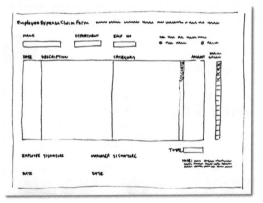

> We have placed the employee details together at the top of the form, while all of the expense information is grouped together in a table—we'll show you how to do this later. Grouping related items together will make your forms more legible and 'user-friendly.'

To create and save a new publication

1 In PagePlus, click **File**, point to **New**, click **New from Startup Wizard**, and then click **Start New Publication**.

2 In the dialog, click **Regular/Normal**, and then click Landscape. Choose an A4 or Letter template, and then click **Open**.

3 Click 💾 **Save**, and save the file as **ExpenseForm.ppp**.

We'll now add the title of our form using a standard text frame.

To add and format a title

1 On the Tools toolbar, click the 📄 **Standard Text Frame** tool, then click and drag to insert a frame in the top left corner of the page.

2 In the text frame, type "Employee Expense Claim Form," and then click the text frame to select it.

3 On the Text context toolbar, choose the font size and style for your title (we've used a 14 pt sans serif font), and click the **B** **Bold** button.

4 With the frame still selected, ensure that the 🔺 **Text** button on the **Swatches** tab is highlighted. From the ▦ **Palette flyout** select the Standard RGB colour set and choose a dark blue swatch.

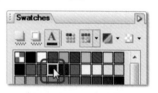

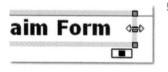

5 If necessary, resize the text frame to fit the text—click one of the frame handles, hold down the left mouse button, and then drag to the new position.

The next step is to add the employee details: name, department, and employee number. It makes sense to include the reimbursement method in this group too. We want these four objects to sit beneath the form title, about 3 cm or so from the top of the page. We can use ruler guides to help us position the items initially. We'll also make use of PagePlus's alignment feature for fine-tuning.

> 🛈 For more information on creating and user ruler and other layout guides, see the section in online Help and the tutorial **Creating Grid Layouts**.

PagePlus lets you set up horizontal and vertical ruler guides—non-printing red lines used to position layout elements.

To create and move ruler guides

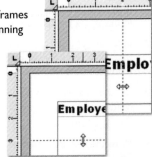

1 Making sure you do not have any text frames selected, click and drag on the ruler running along the top of the page. The dotted red ruler guide line appears.

2 Drag to position the ruler guide at the 3 cm mark. The dotted line changes to solid red.

3 Making sure you do not have any text frames selected, click on the ruler at the left of the page and drag to insert a vertical guide 2 cm from the page edge.

Before continuing, let's check that **snapping** is turned on. This will ensure that any objects we create, move, or resize will jump to align with our ruler guides.

> If a text object is selected, clicking within the object's ruler region adds a tab stop, clicking and dragging elsewhere on the ruler creates a ruler guide.

To turn snapping on or off

• Click the 🔲 **Snapping** button at the right of the Hintline toolbar. When the button is down (i.e. highlighted orange), snapping is on.

When you are happy with the position of your ruler guides, move on to the next section and add the form field labels to the 'employee details' section of the form.

> The snapping feature simplifies placement and alignment by 'magnetizing' grid dots and guide lines. When snapping is on, the edges and centres of objects you create, move, or resize will jump to align with the nearest visible grid dot or guide line. Objects normally snap to the page edge, too.
>
> **To set which visible elements are snapped to:**
>
> 1 Choose **Options** from the **Tools** menu.
>
> 2 On the **Layout** tab, in the **Snap to** section, clear any elements you don't want to snap to.

To add and format form field labels

1 On the Tools toolbar, click the  **Standard Text Frame** tool, then click and drag to insert a text frame at the top left of the page.

> When choosing labels you should make them as clear and meaningful as possible.

2 In the text frame, type "Name," and then click and drag to select the text (or press **Ctrl+A**).

3 On the Text context toolbar, choose the font size and style for your heading (we've used the same font as before but 10 pt size), and click the **B** **Bold** button.

4 With the text still selected, on the **Swatches** tab, choose the same dark blue swatch as before.

   If necessary, resize the text frame to fit the text and then drag to the new position at the point where the ruler guides intersect.

Now that you have created the first form field label, you can use it as a template for the others. This will ensure that all labels are the same height, making it easier for you to align them. Let's use 'copy and paste' to make the other labels for our employee details section.

To copy and paste an object

1 Right-click the object and click **Copy**.

2 Right-click again and click **Paste**.

3 Repeat steps 1 and 2 to create the 'Department,' 'Employee No.' and 'Reimbursement requested by:' labels, adjusting the length of the text frames accordingly.

4 Position the labels by 'snapping' them to the ruler guide, as illustrated.

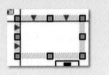

The red triangles pointing towards the ruler guide indicate that the object is 'snapped'. See online Help for more information.

We've laid the groundwork for our first form fields, so now let's create them.

We'll use the Form toolbar for this exercise, but you can also click **Insert > Form Field**. The Form toolbar is a floating toolbar, which you can drag to any position in the PagePlus workspace.

To view the Form toolbar

• On the **View** menu, click **Toolbars** and then click **Form**.

The buttons on the toolbar represent the form field types available. For our first field—Employee Name—we want users to type in their names, so it makes sense to use a **text field** here.

To create a text field

1 On the Form toolbar, click the
   ⬚ **Text Field** button.

2 Move the cursor just below the
   'Name' label and click once to insert
   the field.

We now have a basic text field. As it stands, this field is usable—that is, if we were to publish the form as a PDF, we would be able to type into this box. However, we can change the way a form field looks and behaves by editing its properties.

Text fields

Use a text field when you want the user to type their input—this can be textual or numerical. For example, names, addresses, phone numbers, e-mail addresses, or cash amounts.

We'll use the **Form Field Properties** dialog to:

- Give a unique name to the field.
- Add a ToolTip.
- Format the line around the text box, and the text that the user types into the box.
- Limit the number of letters that can be typed into the box.

To set text field properties

1 Right-click the field, and then click **Form Field Properties** (or double-click the field).

2 On the **General** tab:

- Overwrite the current **Name** with your own name for this field (spaces are not permitted). This name will serve as unique identifier for the field; so it should be descriptive. We used 'Employee_Name.'

- In the **ToolTip** box, type a brief sentence telling the user what information they should type in this field.

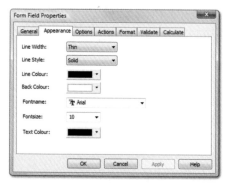

3 On the **Appearance** tab:

- Change the **Line Style** to 'Solid.'

- Choose the format of the user-typed text by selecting values from the **Fontname** and **Fontsize** drop-down lists.

4   On the **Options** tab:

• The **Default Text:** box contains text that is displayed in the form field when the form user first opens the PDF form. We want our fields to be blank, so leave this box empty.

• Select the **Limit Length** check box, and in the box to the right of this option, type '35.' This limits the number of characters allowed to be typed to 35, which should be sufficient for most names.

• Clear the **Scrollable** and **Spell check** boxes.

5   We don't need to change anything on the other tabs, so click **OK** to close the **Form Field Properties** dialog.

Our next form field, 'Department,' is slightly different. Rather than having users type their information into a text box, we want them to be able to select a value from a list. This sounds complicated, but it isn't. We can easily do this with a **combo box**.

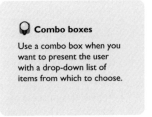

Combo boxes

Use a combo box when you want to present the user with a drop-down list of items from which to choose.

In this case, we want to present employees with a list of departments. We'll create list items for Accounting, Sales, Human Resources, Shipping, and Customer Service.

To create a combo box

1   On the Form toolbar, click the **Combo Box** button.

2   Move the cursor just below the 'Department' label and click once to insert the field.

To set the properties of a combo box

1 Right-click the combo box, and click **Form Field Properties**.

2 On the **General** tab:

- Overwrite the **Name** with your own identifier. We used 'Employee_Department.'

- In the **ToolTip** box, type a brief sentence telling the user what information they should enter in this field. For example, "Click the arrow and select your department."

3 On the **Appearance** tab:

- Change the **Line Style** to 'Solid.'

- In the **Fontname** and **Fontsize** drop-down lists, choose the format for the text that will be displayed in the combo box list.

  You can choose any font, but your form will look better if you use a standard font style throughout. We suggest you select the same font you used for your text field.

4 Click the **Options** tab. You'll notice that it looks different than the **Options** tab for our text field. This is where we add our combo box list items.

- In the **Item** box, type 'Accounting,' and click **Add**. 'Accounting' appears in the **Item** list box.

- Repeat this process to add 'Sales,' 'IT,' 'Human Resources,' 'Shipping,' and 'Customer Service' to the list.

- Select the **Sort items** check box to sort the menu items alphabetically.

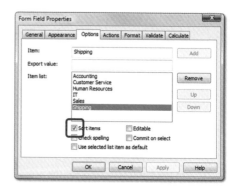

5 We don't need to change anything on the other tabs so click **OK** to close the dialog.

We'll look at the 'Employee No.' field next.

In our fictitious company, assume that employee numbers consist of two letters followed by three numbers—for example, JB007. We want to ensure that employees type this exact format, so we need to somehow validate the data entered. PagePlus PDF forms allow you to validate form data in two different ways, both by means of the **Validate** tab in the **Form Field Properties** dialog:

Simple validation—Use this for numeric fields to restrict the number range that users can enter by setting minimum and maximum values. We'll demonstrate this later.

Custom validation—This more advanced validation can be applied to text fields and editable combo boxes and requires use of JavaScript code. We'll use an example of JavaScript code to validate our 'Employee No.' field.

To denote a particular list item as the 'default' value, select the item in the **Item list:** box, and then click **Use selected list item as default**.

To allow users to enter their own items rather than selecting one from the predefined list, select the **Editable** check box.

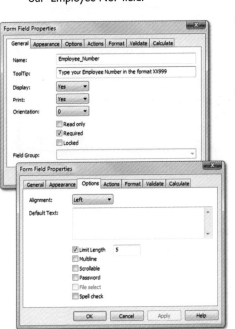

- Follow the steps outlined previously in "To create a text field" to add a text field below the 'Employee No.' label.

- Follow the steps outlined in the "To set the properties of a text field" section to set the properties on the **General** and **Appearance** tabs.

  Your ToolTip should tell the user that they must enter the correct format.

- On the **Options** tab, set the **Limit Length** value to **5**.

We're now ready to add the validation.

To add a custom validation script

1   In the **Form Field Properties** dialog, on the **Validate** tab:

  • Click **Custom validation script**.

  • In the **Custom validation script** box, type the following JavaScript code *exactly*:

```
var str = event.value;
if(!str.match("^[A-Z][A-Z][0-9]+$"))
{
app.alert("Type your Employee Number in the format XX999");
}
```

This code checks that users have typed the correct format, and presents them with an error message if they have not.

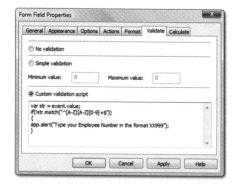

2   Click **OK** to close the **Form Field Properties** dialog.

The development of JavaScript code is beyond the scope of this project. For more information, including the *Acrobat JavaScript Scripting Reference Guide*, go to http://partners.adobe.com/public/developer/pdf/topic_js.html

Some custom JavaScript may not be supported by certain versions of Acrobat Reader. You should test all forms in the Acrobat software used by your target audience.

For the 'Reimbursement Method' field, we could ask users to type their preferred method into a text field, or select it from a list.

There is another type of form field, however, that is particularly suited to this type of data: the **radio button**.

We want employees to choose one of two reimbursement methods—direct deposit or cheque. We'll create a radio button for each option.

Radio buttons

Use radio buttons when you want the user to select a single mutually-exclusive option from a group of two or more options—Yes/No, Often/Sometimes/Never, etc.

To create a radio button

1 On the Form toolbar, click ⊙ **Radio Button**.

2 Move the cursor below the 'Reimbursement requested by:' label, click once to add the field.

3 Repeat to insert a second button.

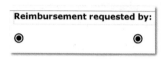

Great, we've created our radio buttons. Now we need to set their properties.

To set the properties of a radio button

1 Double-click the left radio button to open the **Form Field Properties** dialog.

2 On the **General** tab:

- In the **Name** box, replace 'Radio1' with 'Direct_Deposit.'

- In the ToolTip box, type a brief sentence telling users how to use this field. For example, "Select this option to have your expenses reimbursed directly into your bank account."

- At the bottom of the General tab, in the Field Group box, delete 'Radio1,' and replace it with a new group name— Reimbursement_Method.'

The **Field Group** option is unique to radio buttons. To operate correctly, radio buttons that are intended to be grouped must belong to the same field group. We've just created a new 'Reimbursement Method' group, which will contain both of our radio buttons.

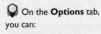 On the **Options** tab, you can:

- Change the style of your radio button—choose from Circle, Check, Cross, Diamond, Star, or Square.

- Select **Checked by default** if you want the radio button to display as selected when the user opens the form.

3 On the **Appearance** tab, change the **Fontsize** to 10 pt.

4 Click **OK** to close the Form Field Properties dialog.

5 Repeat the previous steps to set the properties for the second radio button:

- Name the button 'Cheque.'

- Add an appropriate ToolTip, e.g., "Select this option to have your expenses reimbursed by cheque."

- Add the button to the 'Reimbursement_Method' field group by selecting it from the drop-down list.

- Change the font size to 10 pt.

We've made and configured our radio buttons, now we need to label them appropriately.

1 On the Tools toolbar, click the ▣ **Standard Text Frame** tool, then click and drag to insert a frame to the right of the first radio button.

2 In the text frame, type "Direct deposit," and then click and drag to select the text (or press **Ctrl+A**).

3 On the Text context toolbar, choose the font size and style for your label (we've used a 10 pt sans serif font), and click the **B** **Bold** button to bold the text.

4 Repeat these steps to create a second label for the 'Cheque' radio button.

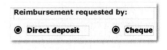

Our employee details form fields and labels are in place, but the form would look better if the objects were aligned. PagePlus provides a precise method of aligning objects on a page using the **Align** tab.

💡 Precise alignment is one key to professional layout. Use menu commands or the **Align** tab to align the edges of any two or more objects with one another; space them out at certain intervals; or align objects with a page margin.

To align objects using the Align tab

1 Press and hold down the **Shift** key, then use the ⬆ **Pointer** tool to click on each of the four label text objects—'Name,' 'Department,' 'Employee No.,' and 'Reimbursement requested by.'

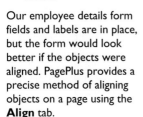

2 On the **Align** tab, click ▣ **Top**. If necessary, clear the **Include margins** checkbox.

3 Repeat step 1 to select all the form fields, including the radio buttons and their labels.

4 On the **Align** tab, click ▣ **Centre Vertically**.

All of the text objects and form fields are now precisely aligned at the top of our page.

Our employee details section is complete. Let's now move on to the expenses section.

We want to present this section of the form in tabular format. We'll begin by adding a ruler guide, then we'll add five text frames for our form field labels. These labels will act as the column headings for our expenses table.

To create and align column headings

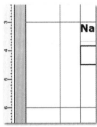

1   Click on the horizontal ruler, and drag down to add a ruler guide at the 6 cm mark.

2   On the Tools toolbar, click the 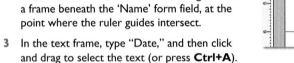 **Standard Text Frame** tool, then click and drag to insert a frame beneath the 'Name' form field, at the point where the ruler guides intersect.

3   In the text frame, type "Date," and then click and drag to select the text (or press **Ctrl+A**).

4   On the Text context toolbar, choose the font size and style for your heading (we've used a black 10 pt sans serif font), and click the **B Bold** button to bold the text.

5   Using this text object as a template, copy and paste it to create text frames for the 'Description,' 'Category,' Amount,' and 'Receipt attached' labels.

6   Position the labels as illustrated.

7   If necessary, use the process described previously to align the column headings.

Our column headings are in place so we're ready to make our table. We'll use a few different types of form fields here—**text fields** for Date, Description, and Amount; a combo box for Category; and a check box for Receipt attached. We'll create the first row of our table and then copy and paste it to create the others. We'll summarize procedures that we've already explained, but go back and refresh your memory if you need to.

To create a text field and set its properties

1   On the Form toolbar, click the
    ⬚ **Text Field** button and insert a
    text field under the 'Date' label.

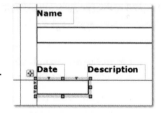

2   Right-click the text field, and click
    Form Field Properties (or double-
    click the field).

3   On the **General** tab:

    • Overwrite the **Name** text with your own identifier.

    • Add the following ToolTip: "Type the date of the expense in the
      format dd/mm/yyyy." (You'll understand why in a minute.)

4   On the **Appearance** tab:

    • Change the **Line Style** to 'Solid.'

    • Choose the format of the user-typed text (we used 10 pt Arial).

5   On the **Options** tab:

    • Clear the **Default Text** box.

    • Select the **Limit Length** check box, and type '10' in the box.

    • Clear all other options.

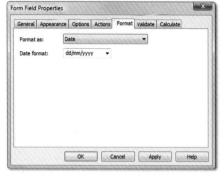

6   On the **Format** tab:

    • In the **Format as** drop-
      down list, select **Date**.

    • In the **Date format** list,
      select **dd/mm/yyyy**
      (now our ToolTip makes
      sense!). Click **OK**.

7   Repeat these steps to
    create two more text
    fields for 'Description' and
    'Amount,' and then
    position them under their
    respective labels.

8 Right-click the 'Description' text field, click **Form Field Properties** and make the following changes:

- On the **General** tab, type a name and an appropriate ToolTip for this field.

- On the **Appearance** tab, select a **Solid** line style and choose the font name and size you used for your 'Date' field.

- On the **Options** tab, delete the default text, set the **Limit Length** to 50, and clear all other options.

9 Right-click the 'Amount' text field, click **Form Field Properties** and make the following changes:

- On the **General** tab, type a name and an appropriate ToolTip.

- On the **Appearance** tab, select a solid line style; choose the font name and size you used for your 'Date' field.

- On the **Options** tab, in the **Alignment** list, select 'Right.' Clear all other options.

- On the **Format** tab:

  - **Format as:** Number
  - **Decimal places:** 2
  - **Separator style:** 9,999.99
  - **Currency symbol:** None
  - **Negative numbers:** Use red text

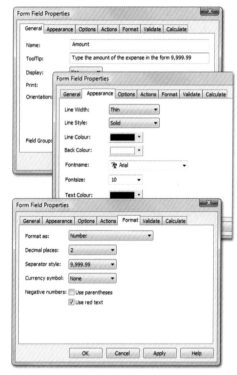

Our text fields are in place, but we still need to align them. Before we do this, let's create the form fields for 'Category' and 'Receipt attached.' We can then group all of these expense form fields and align them in one step. We'll use a combo box for the expense category

> There are a variety of different types of form fields, some of which we will cover in this project. For in-depth information and a list of all the form field types, see "How to create PDF Forms" in online Help.

because we want our users to select a category from a predefined list—Accommodation, Entertainment, Meals, Supplies, Telephone, Travel, and Other. (We have already created a combo box for the 'Department' field so the process will be familiar to you.)

To create a combo box and set its properties

1 On the Form toolbar, click the ▣ **Combo Box** button and add a combo box under the 'Category' label.

2 Right-click the combo box and click **Form Field Properties**.

On the **General** tab:

- Overwrite the current **Name** with your own unique identifier. We used 'ExpenseCategory1.'

- Add the following ToolTip: "Click the arrow and select an expense category."

On the **Appearance** tab:

- Change the **Line Style** to 'Solid.'

- Choose the format of the list box text (we used 10 pt Arial).

On the **Options** tab:

- In the **Item** box, type 'Accommodation,' and then click **Add**.

- Repeat this process to add 'Entertainment,' 'Meals,' 'Supplies,' 'Telephone,' 'Travel,' and 'Other' to the list.

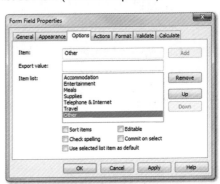

- In this case, don't select the **Sort items** check box because we don't want the list items sorted alphabetically—we want 'Other' to appear at the bottom of our list.

- We don't need to change anything on the other tabs, so click **OK** to close the **Form Field Properties** dialog.

Our last item is 'Receipt attached.' We want to know if the user is attaching a receipt for a particular expense. The best choice for this field is the **check box**.

To create a check box

1 On the Form toolbar, click the ☒ **Check Box** button.

2 Move the cursor just below and to the right of the 'Receipt attached' label. Click once to insert the field.

To set the properties of a check box

1 Right-click the check box, and then click **Form Field Properties.**

2 On the **General** tab:

- Overwrite the current **Name** with your own unique identifier. We used 'Receipt1.'

- In the **ToolTip** box, type "Click this box if you are attaching receipt."

3 On the **Appearance** tab:

- Change the **Line Style** to 'Solid.'

- In the **Fontsize** drop-down list, choose the size you used for your other form fields.

Receipt attached

💡 **Check boxes**

Check boxes are boxes containing a simple check, cross, or other symbol. The form user clicks once to select or clear the box. Check boxes are great for simple Yes/No questions, such as "Do you want to be notified of any upcoming events in the future?" They are also ideal when you want your users to be able to multiple-select a series of options displayed side by side. For example, "Check all the events that are of interest to you."

4   On the **Options** tab:

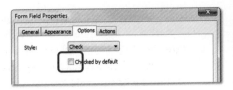

• In the **Style** drop-down
    list, select the style you
    want to use for your
    check box.

• Leave the **Checked by default** box cleared. (If you select this
    option, the check box will appear 'checked' when users first open
    the form, i.e., they'll have to click to clear the box.)

• Click **OK** to close the **Form Field Propertie**s dialog.

You should now have all of your expense form fields in place. We'll now
use the **Align** and **Transform** tabs to align the top row of our expenses
table.

To size and align the objects

1   Select the text box beneath the
    'Date' label.

2   On the **Transform** tab, ensure that
    the ⸙ **Lock Aspect Ratio** is off.

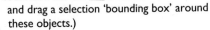

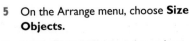

3   Set the Height to 0.65 cm.

4   With the 'Date' text box still
    selected, press and hold down the **Shift** key, then use the ⭦ **Pointer**
    tool to click to select the 'Date' text field, the 'Description' text field,
    the 'Category' combo box, the 'Amount' text field, and the 'Receipt
    attached' check box. (You could also use the ⭦ **Pointer** tool to click
    and drag a selection 'bounding box' around
    these objects.)

5   On the Arrange menu, choose **Size
    Objects**.

6   In the **Size Objects** dialog, select
    Same Vertical Size and click **OK**.
    Your objects should now be the
    same height.

7   On the **Align** tab, click ▣ **Top**.

Finally, we need to get the first four field to line up neatly as if they were part of a table.

8 **Shift**-click to select the 'Date' text field, the 'Description' text field, the 'Category' combo box and the 'Amount' text field objects using the **Pointer** tool.

9 On the **Align** tab, select the **Spaced** option and set it to -0.03 cm (to allow some overlap). Click **Space Evenly Across**.

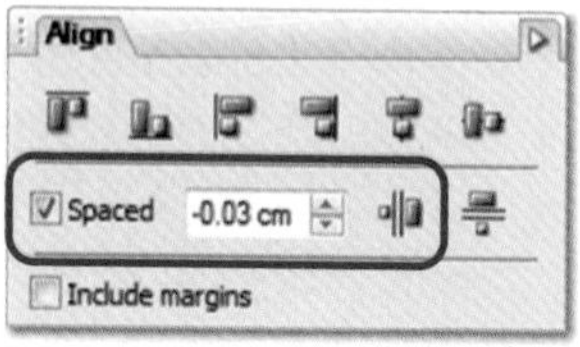

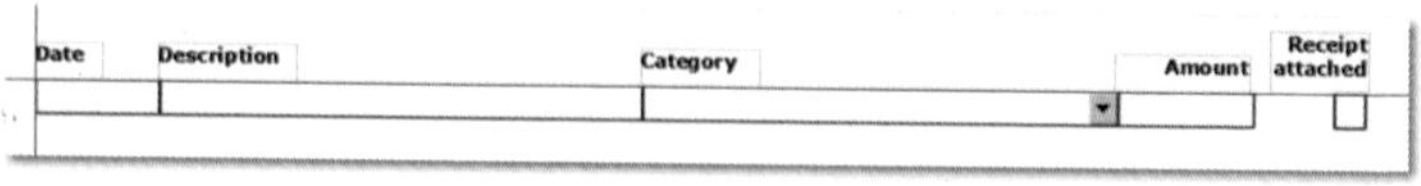

Great, all the hard work is done! Now that our form fields are aligned, we can use this row as a template for the rest of our table.

However, before we continue, we'll show you another useful PagePlus feature—**grouping.**

To create a group from a multiple selection

1 **Shift**-click to select all of the form fields in the row.

2 Click the **Group** button below the selection.

When objects are grouped, you can position, resize, or rotate them all at the same time, just like a single object.

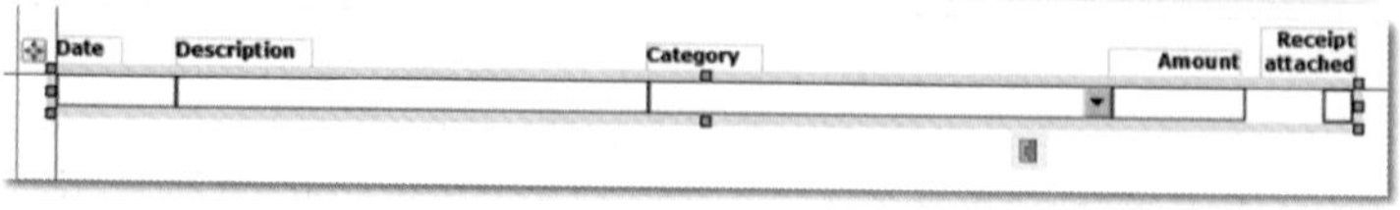

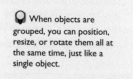

We're now ready to replicate our group and create the rest of our expenses table.

To replicate a group of objects

1 Click on the group of form fields to select them.

2 On the **Edit** menu, click **Replicate...**

3 In the **Replicate** dialog:

- Select **Create grid**.

- Select **Grid size** and set it to 1 x 16.

- Select **Gap** and set the **Horizontal** and **Vertical** values to -0.03 cm

- Ensure **Absolute** is checked.

- Click **OK**.

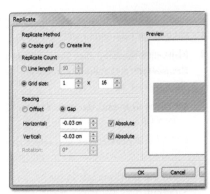

Date	Description	Category	Amount	Receipt attached

That's it, the table is finished! Now all we have to do is create the 'Total' field, and the signature and date text frames.

Let's get the tricky part over with first—creating the 'Total' field. We don't want the user to type into this field. Instead, we want the field to do all the work and automatically add up all the values that appear in the 'Amount' fields.

This may sound complicated, but it isn't. We'll use the **Calculate** tab in the **Form Field Properties** dialog to do this.

To create a calculated field

1 On the Form toolbar, click the **Text Field** button and insert a text field below the last 'Amount' field.

2 Using the Transform tab, resize the new field to be 0.65 cm high—then drag to the new position using the ⊹ **Move** button.

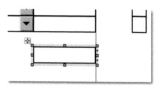

3   Right-align the field with the 'Amount' column. (A ruler guide will help you.)

4   Right-click the field, click **Form Field Properties** and make the following changes:

- On the **General** tab, type a name for this field. (You don't need a ToolTip.)

- On the **Appearance** tab, select a solid line style, and the font name and size you want to use in this field.

- On the **Options** tab, in the **Alignment** list, select 'Right'; clear the default text and all other options.

- On the **Format** tab:

- **Format as:** Number

- **Decimal places:** 2

- **Separator style:** 9,999.99

- **Currency symbol:** Pound (£)

- **Negative numbers:** Use red text

5   Now click the **Calculate** tab.

The last time we used this tab, we created a custom calculation script to check user input. This time, we'll use **simple calculation** instead.

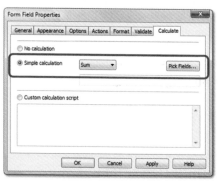

Don't worry, no JavaScript required here! PagePlus will do all the hard work for us, all we need to do is tell it which fields to work with.

6   Click the **Simple calculation** radio button, select **Sum** from the drop-down list, and then click **Pick Fields**.

7 In the **Pick Fields** dialog, hold down the **Shift** key and then click to highlight all of the 'Amount' fields. Scroll down the list to make sure you have selected all 16 fields. Click **OK**.

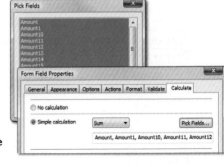

8 The list of fields is now displayed on the **Calculate** tab, under the **Sum** box. Click **OK** to close the **Form Field Properties** dialog.

That's all there is to it. We've created our 'Total' field and just need to label it.

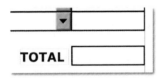

9 Click the **Standard Text Frame** tool and add a text frame to the left of the 'Total' field. Type "TOTAL" in the frame and format the text appropriately using the Context toolbar.

10 Repeat the previous step to add text frames for the employee and manager signatures and dates. Position and align these objects at the bottom of the form.

Use the **Zoom** tools to help you fine-tune the positioning of objects on the page.

Zoom Tool—Click the button, then drag out a rectangular bounding box to define a region to zoom in to. The zoom percentage adjusts accordingly, fitting the designated region into the window. To zoom out, hold down the **Shift** key when dragging. Double-click the button to display the page at actual size (100%).

Zoom Out—Click to view more of the page in the window.

Zoom In—Click to view the page area more closely.

On our form that we have two 'notes'—one at the top of the form and another at the bottom (created with standard text frames). Obviously these aren't mandatory. However, wherever possible, you should aim to provide any additional information that might help the user complete the form.

Everything is in place, we've finished laying out our form. Before we publish it as a PDF form, there are a couple of small but important tasks we should do—set the **tab order** of the form fields, and **lock** the form objects.

Navigating the form

Our form users can navigate through the form fields in one of two ways—they can use the mouse and click each field in turn; or they can use the **Tab** key to jump from field to field. As forms are generally designed to be completed in sequential manner, 'tabbing' is considered the more efficient method. In addition, it's important to set a logical tab order so that users who are unable to use a mouse can complete the form easily.

The tab order is governed by the order in which the form designer adds the form fields to the page. As the form design may change during the design process, the tab order may be thrown out of sequence.

Fortunately, the 🔲 **Tab Order** button on the Form toolbar can be used to reset the tab order at the end of the design process. In this project, we added our form fields in the order in which we want our users to complete them. Because of this, you'll see that our tab order is already logically sequenced. For demonstration purposes, however, we'll show you how this feature works so you can make use of it in the future.

Note: Tab order can only be set on ungrouped fields. If any fields are grouped at the time of pressing the 🔲 **Tab Order** button, a warning dialog will appear. Just click **OK** to ungroup the fields.

> PagePlus
>
> ⓘ Grouped fields must be ungrouped before the Tab Order can be set. Would you like to ungroup them now?
>
> OK   Cancel

To change tab order

1   On the Form toolbar, click the 🔲 **Tab Order** button. This reveals blue tab markers on all your form fields.

2 Click on the form fields in
   the order in which you
   want them to be assigned
   tab numbers. PagePlus
   automatically assigns a
   new tab number to the
   blue marker.

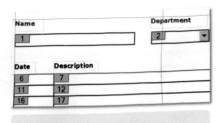

3 Click the **Tab Order**
   button again to switch off
   the blue tab markers.

> To reset the tab order, click the **Tab Order** button and start again.

It has taken lot of time and effort to set up our form layout and tab order,
so let's lock our form objects to prevent us from accidentally moving
them.

We're going to lock all the objects on the form, but you can use the
following procedure for single or multiple objects.

To lock objects

1 On the **Edit** menu, click **Select**, and
   then click **Select All** (or use the
   Pointer tool to draw a selection
   bounding box around all of the
   objects on the page).

2 Right-click the selection, click
   Arrange, and then click **Lock
   Objects**.

3 Now click on one of your form fields
   and try to move it.

To unlock objects

• Right-click the object(s), then click
  Arrange > Unlock Objects.

We're finally ready to save our form and publish it to PDF format.

You can export any PagePlus publication as a PDF file—not just forms. This project covers the basic steps and options. For more information, see "Exporting PDF files" in online Help.

To publish a PDF form

1 On the **File** menu, click **Publish as PDF**.

2 On the **General** tab, in the **Compatibility** drop-down list, select the appropriate Acrobat version.

3 Select the **Preview PDF file in Acrobat** check box, and then click **OK**.

4 In the **Publish to PDF** dialog, type a file name for the PDF, and save it in a convenient location.

   The **Publish to PDF** dialog closes and your form opens in Adobe Acrobat.

Your work is not finished yet—you still need to check your form to make sure that it works in the way you expect.

When checking your form, you should:

● Check the tab order.

● Hover over the form fields and make sure that ToolTips are spelled correctly.

● Make sure you can type into all text fields.

● Check that all fields are long enough to hold the typed text or predefined list item.

> 🔋 PDF is a cross-platform file format, developed by Adobe, which has evolved into a worldwide standard for document distribution. PDF files work equally well for electronic or paper publishing—including professional printing. In recent years, print shops are moving away from PostScript and toward the newer, more reliable PDF/X formats expressly targeted for graphic arts and high quality reproduction. Several different "flavours" of PDF/X exist; PagePlus supports PDF/X-1 and PDF/X-1a.

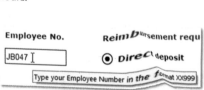

- Check the entries in the combo box drop-down lists—are the items spelled correctly, does all of the text display properly?

- Make sure that you can't select more than one radio button in a group

- Verify that any calculated fields work correctly—if not, you've probably entered the wrong calculation type, or the wrong fields on the **Calculate** tab.

- Check any validation—e.g., make sure that incorrect data is not accepted and generates an error message.

Well done! You've designed a business expense form from start to finish, and you've published it to PDF format. You can now post the PDF form on your company intranet and let your users take it for a test run! (Of course, you've already tested it thoroughly so there shouldn't be any surprises.)

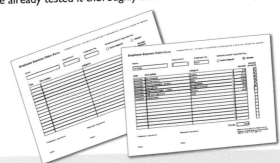

If you don't want to create your own PDF form from scratch, you can start with a PagePlus template and then modify it to suit your needs.

1 From the Startup Wizard, click **Use Design Template**.

2 Under **Desktop Printing**, the **PDF Forms** category contains a selection of form types and styles.

3 Choose a template and click **Open**.

4 You can now add, edit, and delete text objects, graphics, and form fields as required to create your own custom form.

Creating a Sales Flyer

Whether you're selling your car, organizing an event, or opening a new business, a flyer is an easy to produce, inexpensive, yet effective marketing tool.

In this project, you'll create a 'Car for Sale' flyer from scratch. You can use your own images or the sample images provided in your **...\Tutorials\Workspace\Sales Flyer** folder. In a standard installation, you'll find this folder in the following location:

C:\ProgramFiles\Serif\PagePlus\X3

In this exercise, you'll learn how to:

- Create frame and artistic text.
- Apply text formatting and adjust text leading.
- Apply a shadow filter effect to heading text.
- Import, position, resize, and crop images.
- Adjust image brightness and contrast.
- Create and position QuickShapes.
- Adjust line and border properties.
- Apply a transparency effect to a shape.
- Preview and print a publication.

Creating a Sales Flyer

In this project, we'll assume that you're selling your car from home, and that you'll be printing your flyer on A4 or Letter sized paper, on a home printer. If you want to use your own images, they should be clear and should show the car from different angles.

We'll start by creating and saving a blank document. We'll insert a standard text frame, type a headline, apply some basic text formatting, and create a drop shadow filter effect.

To create and save a new publication

1   In PagePlus, click **File**, point to **New**, click **New from Startup Wizard**, and then click **Start New Publication**.

2   In the dialog, click **Regular/Normal**, and then click **Portrait**. Click the **A4** or **Letter** template, and then click **Open**.

3   To save your new document, click **File** then **Save**. Save the file as **CarForSale.ppp**.

We want our heading to grab the reader's attention, so we need to make it large and bold. You can use any font style you like, but it's generally best to use a sans serif font for headings.

To create a heading using artistic text

1   On the Tools toolbar, click the A ▾ **Artistic Text** tool, click in the top left corner of the page and type "FOR SALE."

2   Triple-click the text object to select both words (or press **Ctrl+A**).

3   On the **Text** context toolbar, choose the font size and style for your heading.

FOR SALE

| Normal ▾ | *Basic* Sans Heavy SF ▾ | 160 pt ▾ |

4   Click between the words for an insertion point, and then press the **Enter** key to place each on a separate line.

Next, we'll adjust the leading—the distance from one line of text to the ext.

You can use the **Fonts** tab to view your currently installed fonts and apply them to your text objects.

Select your text, then hover over a listed font for an in-place preview—if you like what you see, simply click to apply the font to your text.

The tab also hosts a **quick search** feature to filter fonts by name, attribute, or type.

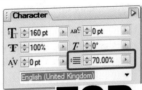

To adjust text leading

- Select the text, then on the **Character** tab, change the leading value to '70%.'

Our headline words now sit snugly one on top of the other.

PagePlus provides a variety of filter effects, which you can use to transform any object. We can make our headline text stand out even more by applying a diffused shadow.

To apply a drop shadow

1 Select the text frame.

2 On the **Styles** tab, in the drop-down category list, select **Shadows**.

3 Select an appropriate drop shadow from the **Drop Shadow** sub-category.

4 Click on the thumbnail to apply the effect.

The **Styles** tab provides predefined styles that you can apply to objects, or customize to suit your own taste. Each object style can include settings for multiple attributes such as line colour, line style, fill, transparency, filter effects, font, and border. See "Using object styles" in online Help.

Now for the photographs of the car. We'll use four different images for this flyer. They'll need some adjustment though. In these next steps, we'll be resizing, cropping, and adjusting brightness and contrast levels.

To import and resize an image

1. Click outside the text frame to deselect it. On the Tools toolbar, click **Import Picture**.
2. In the **Import Picture** dialog, browse to the ...**Workspace\Sales Flyer** folder and open the **CFSfront.png** file.
3. When the cursor changes to a , click and drag on the page to insert the image. (Note that the Picture context toolbar displays.)
4. Resize and move the image until it fits into the space to the right of the headline.

Notice that this image is a little dark. We'll use the Picture context toolbar to adjust it.

To adjust image brightness and contrast

1. Select the image and the Picture context toolbar displays.
2. To adjust the brightness click:
   - to increase brightness.
   - to decrease brightness.
3. To adjust contrast click:
   - to increase contrast.
   - to decrease contrast.

The **Photo Optimizer** helps you improve the print quality of an image on a specific printer. You can print test samples and choose the best brightness and contrast settings.

With the image selected, on the **Format** menu, click **Picture > Photo Optimizer**, and then follow the instructions in the Wizard.

We'll now insert the main photo for our flyer. We could use the image just as it is. However, there's a lot of background and we're only interested in the car. Let's crop the image, and focus on the car.

To crop an image

1   Repeat steps 1 to 3 of the "To import an image" section to import the **CFSside2.png** file. Resize this image so that it sits beneath the headline and fills the width of the page.

2   With the image selected, on the Attributes toolbar, click the ⊡ **Square Crop** tool.

3   Click the handle in the upper centre of the image and drag down until you have cropped most of the background.

Repeat the process to crop the background on either side of the *car.*

4   Repeat steps 1 to 3 of the "To import and resize an image" *section* to import the **CFSscenery.png** and **CFSside.png** files. Resize these images and position them in the lower right corner of the page, as illustrated.

Great, our images are now in place. They show the car from different angles and give the reader a good idea of its appearance and condition. We'll now insert some text *frames* and add the car's details and *key* selling points.

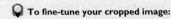 **To fine-tune your cropped image:**

Click in the image (the cursor changes to), and then drag to reposition the image inside the crop boundary. To restore the cropped object to its original shape, click **Remove Crop** on the Crop flyout.

Adding sales text

1 Click the ▣ **Standard Text Frame** tool and insert some text frames in the space at the lower left of the page.

2 Click inside the frames for an insertion point, and then type the car details into the boxes.

You could use just one text frame. We used three, however, to give us more flexibility with positioning—try dragging the frames around the page to experiment with different positions.

Now for the finishing touches. For a fun effect, we'll use a **QuickShape** and a transparency effect to create pieces of sticky tape to 'stick' our main photo to the page.

When working with multiple images, instead of inserting them one at a time, why not add them all to the **Media Bar**. As you work on your document, you can then quickly view the images and drag and drop them onto the page when you need them. You'll find more details in the **How To** tab and in online Help.

We'll now insert the main photo for our flyer. We could use the image just as it is. However, there's a lot of background and we're only interested in the car. Let's crop the image, and focus on the car.

To crop an image

1 Repeat steps 1 to 3 of the "To import an image" section to import the **CFSside2.png** file. Resize this image so that it sits beneath the headline and fills the width of the page.

2 With the image selected, on the Attributes toolbar, click the ⊐ **Square Crop** tool.

3 Click the handle in the upper centre of the image and drag down until you have cropped most of the background.

Repeat the process to crop the background on either side of the car.

4 Repeat steps 1 to 3 of the "To import and resize an image" section to import the **CFSscenery.png** and **CFSside.png** files. Resize these images and position them in the lower right corner of the page, as illustrated.

Great, our images are now in place. They show the car from different angles and give the reader a good idea of its appearance and condition. We'll now insert some text frames and add the car's details and key selling points.

> 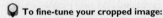 **To fine-tune your cropped image:**
>
> Click in the image (the cursor changes to 🖑), and then drag to reposition the image inside the crop boundary. To restore the cropped object to its original shape, click **Remove Crop** on the Crop flyout.

Adding sales text

1   Click the  **Standard Text Frame** tool and insert some text frames in the space at the lower left of the page.

2   Click inside the frames for an insertion point, and then type the car details into the boxes.

  You could use just one text frame. We used three, however, to give us more flexibility with positioning—try dragging the frames around the page to experiment with different positions.

Now for the finishing touches. For a fun effect, we'll use a **QuickShape** and a transparency effect to create pieces of sticky tape to 'stick' our main photo to the page.

> 💡 When working with multiple images, instead of importing them one at a time, why not add them all to the **Media Bar**. As you work on your document, you can then quickly view your images and drag and drop them onto the page when you need them. You'll find more details in the **How To** tab and in online Help.

To create and format a Quick Shape

1 On the Tools toolbar, on the **Quick Shape** flyout, select the **Quick Rectangle**.

2 Click and drag to create a rectangle about 2 x 0.75 cm.

3 Right-click the rectangle, click **Format**, and then click **Line and Border**.

4 In the **Line and Border** dialog, on the **Line** tab:

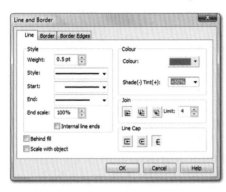

- In the **Weight** box, click '0.5 pt.'

- In the **Shade(-) Tint(+)** box, in the drop-down list, click '+50%.'

- Click **OK**.

We're halfway there—we've created our basic rectangle and lightened its border. To resemble tape, however, our shape has to be transparent.

To add transparency to an object

1 Select the rectangle object.

2 On the **Transparency** tab, click the **Solid** button.

3 Click the **40% Solid Transparency** to apply it to the shape.

> 💡 Transparency effects are great for highlights, shading and shadows, and simulating 'rendered' realism. They can make the critical difference between flat-looking illustrations and images with depth and snap.

Now that we've created the template for our 'tape,' we can copy and paste it to quickly create another three identical shapes.

To copy and paste an object

1 Select the object, right-click, and then click **Copy**.

2 Right-click again and click **Paste**.

3 Repeat steps 1 and 2 to create a total of four identical shapes. The copies will be pasted one on top of the other in the centre of the workspace.

Now all we have to do is position our shapes—we want them to appear to be holding down the corners of our main image. To do this, we need to rotate them.

To rotate an object

1 Click to select the object, hover next to one of the handles —the pointer changes to the **Rotate** cursor—and then drag to rotate the shape.

2 Now click in the centre of the object—the pointer changes to the **Move** cursor—and drag the shape into the desired position.

3 Repeat steps 1 to 3 to rotate and position each of the shapes as illustrated.

That's it! We've finished creating our flyer and are ready to view and print it.

First of all, let's change to Print Preview mode and look at our layout without frames, guides, rulers, and other screen items. As you are designing your PagePlus publications, you might find it useful to occasionally switch to Print Preview mode to give you an idea of how your layout will look on the printed page.

To preview the printed page

- Click the  **Print Preview** button on the Standard toolbar (or on the **File** menu, click **Print Preview**.)

To cancel Print Preview mode

- Click the ✕ **Close Preview** button at the lower edge of the preview window.

Assuming you were happy with the way your flyer previewed, let's go ahead and print it out. For this exercise, you only require basic desktop printer output. However, PagePlus supports scaling, tiling, colour separations, and many other useful printing options. For more information, see "How to Print Your Publication" in online Help.

To print a publication

1   On the **File** menu, click **Print**.

2   In the **Print** dialog, on the **General** tab, do the following:

- Select your desktop printer from the **Name** drop-down list.

- Select the print range to be printed—in this case, we only have a single page, so click **Document**.

- Select the number of copies you want to print.

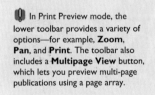

In Print Preview mode, the lower toolbar provides a variety of options—for example, **Zoom**, **Pan**, and **Print**. The toolbar also includes a **Multipage View** button, which lets you preview multi-page publications using a page array.

- Click the **Properties** button to set up the printer for the correct page orientation—**Portrait**.

- **Note:** Depending on your printer driver, to print text with shading or custom settings, you may need to edit the printer properties to set it to "download TrueType fonts as bitmap soft fonts". The location and exact name of this option varies from printer to printer but is often found within the 'Advanced' options of the Printer Properties dialog.

- When you are happy with your printer settings, click **Print**.

> The PagePlus Page design templates include a selection of ready-made flyer publications, which you can customize to suit your needs.
>
> **To use a template:**
>
> Click **File > New > New from Startup Wizard**, then click **Use Design Template**.

Your sales flyer will print in colour on a colour printer or in shades of grey on a black and white printer.

Congratulations, you have successfully created and printed a sales flyer from scratch!

We've covered a lot of ground in this project, and you should now be feeling more familiar with some of PagePlus's powerful desktop publishing tools and features. We hope that you have enjoyed the exercise, and have learned a few things in the process.

What's next? Well, that depends on what you want to do. If you're feeling adventurous and want to try your hand at creating a multi-page publication, see the "Creating a Newsletter" and "Creating a Photo Scrapbook" projects. If you want more hands-on experience with graphic objects, try "Creating a Greetings Card."

Creating a CD Cover
and Label

Whatever type of CD or DVD you're making, you'll find the PagePlus templates a valuable tool to help you create your own custom cover and label designs. In this project, we'll start with a blank template and show you how to combine text and images to create various design solutions.

You'll learn how to:

- Work with a PagePlus CD/DVD template.
- Import and position images.
- Create and resize Quick Shapes.
- Crop images and shapes.
- Create, format, and align text.
- Apply colour fills to text and shapes.
- Create a custom colour fill using a colour taken from an image.
- Use the Pencil tool.
- Create a transparent PNG file.
- Use the Replicate command.
- Preview your design on the printed page.

Creating a CD Cover and Label

In the first section of this project, we'll design a CD-ROM (CD) cover for a classical music collection. We'll base our design on an imported image and add a title. Next, we'll extract the focal point of our cover image and use it to create a simple, but striking label. Our aim is to create two designs which share the same design theme (providing continuity), but which are also strong enough to stand alone. You can use your own images or our sample images, which you'll find in your **...\Tutorials\Workspace\CD** folder. In a standard installation, this folder is installed to the following location:

C:\Program Files\Serif\PagePlus\X3

To conclude we'll show you a few other examples to illustrate various design techniques.

Creating the CD cover and tray insert

We'll begin by designing the CD cover. It's the first thing people will see when they pick up the CD, and it's also a much easier shape to start with than the circular label!

To create the cover design

1   Click **File**, point to **New** and click **New from Startup Wizard**. In the Startup Wizard, select **Start New Publication**.

Expand the **Small Publications** section, then the **Avery** section. In the **CD/DVD Labels** category, click the **CD/DVD Case Cover and Tray J8435** template and then click **Open**.

2   On the Tools toolbar, click the 🖼 ▾ **Import Picture** button. In the **Import Picture** dialog, browse to the **...\Workspace\CD** folder and open the **Violin_1.jpg** file.

3   When the cursor changes to the ⁺🖼 **Import Picture** cursor, click and drag on your page to import the image.

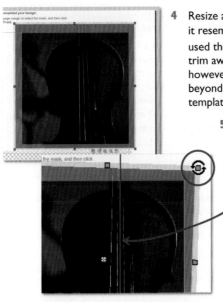

4   Resize and position the image so that it resembles our illustration. (We used the ⬚ ▾ **Square Crop** tool to trim away the edges of the image; however, any areas that extend beyond the blue border of the template will not be printed.)

5   Use the ↻ **Rotate** tool to rotate the image so that the violin strings run in a true vertical line down the page. To help you do this, add a vertical ruler guide to the page (click and drag on the vertical ruler at the left of the page). You can then rotate the image so that the centre of the strings lines up with the ruler guide.

When you are happy with the placement of your image, you can add your title.

6   On the Tools toolbar, click the ▣ ▾ **Standard Text Frame** tool and then drag to create a text frame on top of your image. Type the title of your CD into the frame. Press the **Enter** key each time you want to start a new line.

Let's now set up our frame so that we have a narrow margin all around the edge. Then we'll format our lines of text.

7 With the text frame selected, on the Frame context toolbar, click  **Frame Setup**.

In the **Frame Setup** dialog, enter 0.5 cm in the **Top**, **Bottom**, **Left Margin**, and **Right Margin** value boxes.

You should now see a border of 0.5 cm all around your text frame.

Let's now apply some formatting to the text.

8 To format text, you first need to select it. To do this, you can:

- Click and drag to highlight a line of text.

- Double-click to select a single word.

- Triple-click to select a paragraph.

When you've selected the text you want to format, use the buttons on the Text context toolbar to change font style, size, and alignment.

To change the vertical alignment within the frame, right-click on the text object, then click **Text Format > Vertical Text Alignment > Centre**.

9 Now select the entire text frame. On the **Swatches** tab, click the **A Text** button and then click a white swatch to apply the colour to all of the text inside the frame.

Now we'll apply a background fill to our text frame. For this, we could simply choose a colour from the **Swatches** tab. However, we want to match the red in our image so we'll use the **Colour Picker** to help us do this.

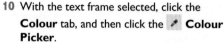

10 With the text frame selected, click the **Colour** tab, and then click the 🖊 **Colour Picker**.

On the image, click and drag to select the colour you want to apply to the background of your text frame.

The popup colour sample updates as you drag to different areas of the image.

When you are happy with the colour displayed in the sample, release the mouse button.

The selected colour is applied to the text frame, and added to the **Publication Palette** on the **Swatches** tab.

11 Resize and position the text frame as illustrated (left) and the front of your CD cover is complete!

Don't worry about the edges of the design. The template is set up to trim these away for you—we'll show you how this works later.

Now for the CD tray insert. We'll start by creating a Quick Shape and applying the same red fill. We'll then import an image, create a track list, and add the CD title to the spine of the insert.

To create the tray insert design

1 On the Tools toolbar, on the QuickShape flyout, click the 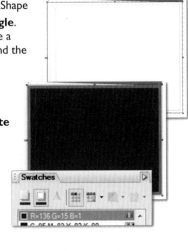 **Quick Rectangle**. Click and drag on the page to create a rectangle that extends slightly beyond the border of the tray insert template.

2 With the shape selected, on the **Swatches** tab:

   • Click the ▦ **Publication Palette** button.

   • Click the ⬜ **Fill** button and then click the red swatch you created in the previous section.

   • Click the ⬜ **Line** button and apply the same colour to the shape's outline.

3 Repeat the steps outlined previously to import the image and create and format the text frames illustrated in the layout below.

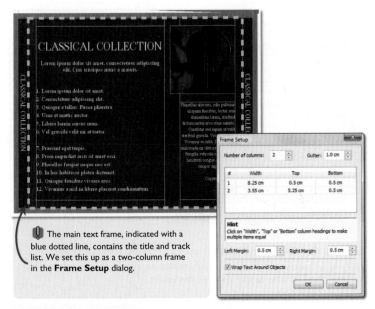

ℹ The main text frame, indicated with a blue dotted line, contains the title and track list. We set this up as a two-column frame in the **Frame Setup** dialog.

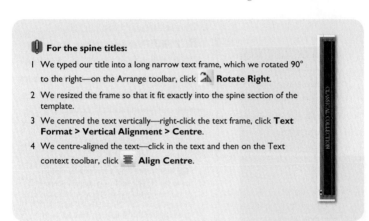

> **ℹ️ For the spine titles:**
>
> 1 We typed our title into a long narrow text frame, which we rotated 90°
>   to the right—on the Arrange toolbar, click 🔺 **Rotate Right**.
>
> 2 We resized the frame so that it fit exactly into the spine section of the
>   template.
>
> 3 We centred the text vertically—right-click the text frame, click **Text
>   Format > Vertical Alignment > Centre**.
>
> 4 We centre-aligned the text—click in the text and then on the Text
>   context toolbar, click ≡ **Align Centre**.

Our design is complete. Now to follow the instructions outlined in blue in
the upper left corner of the template itself.

**To complete, preview, and
print the design**

1 Click on the white page
  margin to select the template
  mask, then on the Arrange
  toolbar, click 📋 **Bring to
  Front**.

  - or -

  On the **Arrange** menu, click
  Bring to Front.

The edges of
the image now
disappear
behind the
mask.

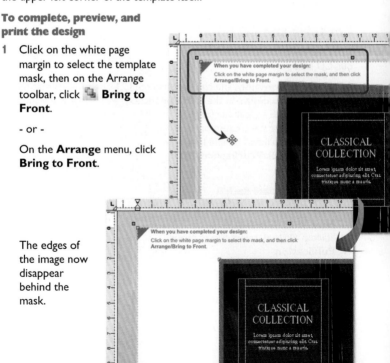

2 On the Standard toolbar, click

📖 **Print Preview** to see how your design will appear on the printed page.

3 If you are happy with your layout, click the 🖨 **Print Publication** button to print out your finished cover and tray insert design.

> 💡 Before printing your design directly onto the Avery labels, we suggest you print it out on normal A4 or Letter sized paper first (you can use Quick Shapes to indicate the edges of the template). This will help you to ensure that your text and images are positioned correctly.

Creating the CD label

With the cover design complete, we'll move on and create the design for our CD label.

As mentioned previously, the circular shape of CD labels means that they can be difficult to design. In the following section, we'll show you a simple method to create a great label that echoes the theme we created on our cover. Again, you'll find sample images in your **...\Tutorials\Workspace\CD** folder.

To create the label design

1 Click **File**, point to **New**, then click **New from Startup Wizard**. In the Startup Wizard, select **Start New Publication**.

Expand the **Small Publications** section, then the **Avery** section. In the **CD/DVD Labels** category, click the **Full Face CD/DVD Labels J8676** template and then click **Open**.

2   On the Tools toolbar, click the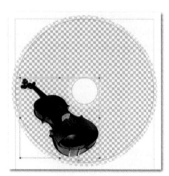
    Import Picture button. In the
    Import Picture dialog, browse to
    the **...\Tutorials\Workspace\CD**
    folder and open the **Violin_2.jpg** file.

3   When the cursor changes to the
    ✛▩ **Import Picture** cursor, click
    and drag on your page to import the
    image.

4   Resize and position the image on the
    template so that it resembles our
    illustration.

5   On the Tools toolbar, use
    the ▣ **Standard Text
    Frame** tool to add text to
    your label.

    Follow the steps outlined
    in the previous section to
    format and apply colour to
    your text. (We didn't want
    our text elements to
    distract focus from the
    image, so we reduced the
    font size.)

6   Click on the white page
    margin to select the
    template mask, then on
    the Arrange toolbar, click
    ▣ **Bring to Front** (or
    click **Arrange** then **Bring
    to Front**).

7   When you are happy with
    your design, click **File**
    then **Print** to print it out.

○ To produce an image with a
transparent background, we imported the
violin image into PagePlus and then used
Image Cutout Studio to remove the
background. For more information about
Image Cutout Studio, see the **How To** tab
and online Help.

You could also remove the background
using photo editing software, such as Serif
PhotoPlus, before importing the image into
PagePlus.

For our finished label design, we isolated the focal point of our CD cover image and placed it on a white background. By doing so, we have achieved continuity and created a bold, but simple statement.

There are many other ways you can place text and images onto your label template to create very different effects.

For example, we could 'bleed' the edge of our image over the label border. This simple change gives quite a different look and feel to our composition.

Or we could produce a different effect by using the cover image along with simple white text.

The following examples illustrate some other design techniques to get you started, but we think you'll have fun experimenting with your own ideas.

Example 1

Here's how we created the design illustrated left:

1   We imported the same image used on the cover, positioning the violin in the centre of the label.

2   On the Tools toolbar, on the QuickShape flyout, we chose the ▢ **Quick Rectangle** and created a rectangle that covered half of the label template.

3   On the **Colour** tab, we used the ✎ **Colour Picker** to sample a shade from our image (see step 10 of the previous "Creating the CD cover and tray insert" section).

    We applied this colour to the fill and outline of our shape.

4   We placed a text frame on top of the shape to complete our design.

5   By bringing the mask to the front, the overlapping areas of the design were hidden from view.

Example 2

In our next example, our design is based on a photo of a collection of keys. If you want to work through the following steps using our images, you'll find them in your **...\Tutorials\Workspace\CD** folder.

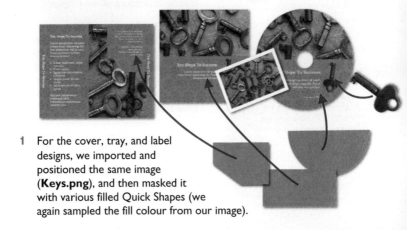

1   For the cover, tray, and label designs, we imported and positioned the same image (**Keys.png**), and then masked it with various filled Quick Shapes (we again sampled the fill colour from our image).

2 The single key was extracted from the main image and then exported to a transparent PNG file (**Single key.png**) using the following technique:

- We imported the **Keys.png** file into a new blank document and cropped it to focus on the key we wanted to extract.

  We then resized the image so that the key was about half the size of the page.

- On the Line flyout, we used the ✎ **Pencil** tool to trace around the outline of the key, making sure to close the shape by joining the first and last nodes (you'll know if you have succeeded in doing this because you'll be able to fill your resulting shape).

- **Optional step:** When we were happy with our outline, we copied and pasted it into a new blank document—we needed another outline to create the background pattern (step 3, below), so wanted to use this copy instead of repeating the tracing procedure all over again!

- We returned to our original document and grouped the inner and outer key outlines. We then selected the outline group and the photograph underneath it. Then, on the **Tools** menu, we clicked **Crop to Shape** to crop to the outline of the key.

🎙 Using the Pencil tool

When tracing around an object, don't worry about being too precise. You can fine-tune your outline afterwards by editing the nodes and smoothing the curves of your outline.

For more information, see "Drawing and editing lines" in online Help.

- On the **File** menu, we clicked **Export As Picture**. In the **Export As Picture** dialog, in the **Save as type** drop-down list, we selected **Portable Network Graphic (*.png)** and ensured that **Show filter options** was checked.

  We named our image and clicked **Save**.

- In the **Portable Network Graphic Format Export Options** dialog, we chose to export as a 24 bit, 150 dpi image, with a transparent background. We then imported our key image into our CD label document.

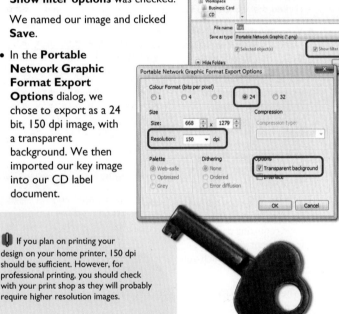

🔋 If you plan on printing your design on your home printer, 150 dpi should be sufficient. However, for professional printing, you should check with your print shop as they will probably require higher resolution images.

3 To create the repeating background pattern (**Background_1.png** and **Background_2.png**), which we laid on top of our Quick Shapes:

- We opened the publication containing the key outline, which we created in the previous section.

- We filled the shape with another colour sampled from our image and exported it as a transparent PNG file, as described in the previous section.

- We copied and pasted the key outline eight times, rotating by increments of 45° each time, until we had achieved the circular pattern illustrated here.

- When we were happy with the arrangement of elements, we selected the entire group and clicked the 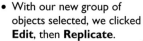 **Group** button.

- With our new group of objects selected, we clicked **Edit**, then **Replicate**.

  In the **Replicate** dialog, we created a diagonal line of designs, then copied and pasted the line.

  We positioned the copied line next to our first line, as illustrated.

  You can use copy and paste or the **Replicate** command to create your repeating pattern. Experiment with both methods to see which you prefer.

  When your design is complete, you can copy and paste it directly onto your CD label document, or you can export the whole thing as a transparent .png and then import it into your document.

- We completed our design with text formatted in white.

The **Replicate** command lets you create multiple copies in a single step, with precise control over how the copies are arranged, either as a linear series or a grid. It's great for repeating backgrounds, or for perfectly-aligned montages of an image or object.

Example 3

Our final example is based on a collection of family photographs, which we cropped and resized on the page to create a montage.

We applied a subtle grey colour to our text so that the focus remains on the images.

That concludes this project!

We hope you have enjoyed working through these exercises, and have learned some new PagePlus techniques along the way. We've illustrated four different design ideas, which you should be able to adapt to suit your own needs and taste. Of course, there are lots more techniques you can use. We hope that our examples will inspire you to experiment with the powerful tools provided in PagePlus, and that you'll go on to create some unique designs of your own.

> For other design ideas, take a look at the PagePlus CD/DVD label templates:
>
> - From the Startup Wizard, click **Use Design Template** and browse the CD/DVD category.

Creating a Ticket Book

In this project, we'll show you a quick and easy way to create simple numbered tickets by using the PagePlus master pages and page numbering features.

You'll learn how to:

- Set up printer and page size options.
- Work with master pages.
- Add page numbers to a master page.
- Align text objects.
- Add pages to a publication.
- Preview a publication on the printed page.
- Prefix page numbers with leading zeros.

Creating a Ticket Book

PagePlus provides a wealth of features to help you create many different publication types. In this simple project, we'll show you a useful way to combine master pages, and page numbering. We'll then demonstrate some of the powerful printing options available to you.

1   Before starting PagePlus you should begin by selecting your printer and page size. In Windows®, go to your **Printers** window (this process differs slightly between versions of Windows), then right-click on your printer of choice and choose **Properties**.

   In the dialog, select a suitable page size. In our example, we will use a desktop inkjet printer and A5 paper (roughly 6" x 8"). Make a comparable choice that's supported by your specific printer.

2   Open PagePlus and in the Startup Wizard, click **Cancel** (in the upper right corner of the window). This will open a default blank page.

   On the Pages context toolbar, click **Page Setup**.

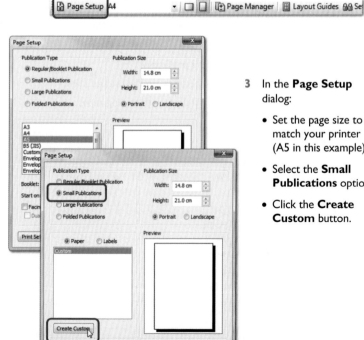

3   In the **Page Setup** dialog:

   - Set the page size to match your printer (A5 in this example).

   - Select the **Small Publications** option.

   - Click the **Create Custom** button.

4   In the **Small Publication Setup** dialog:

- In the **Layout** section, set the gap values, **Gap X** and **Gap Y**, to 0.0 cm.

- Set the **Across value** to **2** and the **Down** value to **5**.

- In the **Margins** section, leave the **Auto** check box selected.

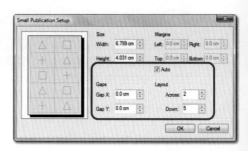

PagePlus automatically calculates the small publication size required to fit this many 'pages' on to the paper size you selected earlier. Selecting the Auto option ensures that PagePlus will not use the unprintable area of your paper in its calculations or printing.

5   Click **OK** once to return to the **Page Setup** dialog. Click **OK** again to return to the PagePlus workspace.

Now your publication size will switch to the new settings. You can ignore the default blue margin indicated—or if you wish, right-click on your page, choose Layout Guides, then set your margins to zero.

6   At the lower left of the workspace, click the **Current Page** box (currently displaying **I of I**) to switch to the master page.

Master pages are background pages, like sheets of extra paper behind your main publication pages. Every page layer can have one master page assigned to it and a given master page can be shared by any number of main pages.

The publication we're working with offers the simplest possible case: a single page with one layer. Objects on the master page show through to the main page (unless they're obscured or you've switched off **Master Page Objects** on the **View** menu).

Placing objects on a master page lets them appear on more than one page—useful for logos, headers, footers and auto-generated page numbers. For an overview of these elements, see "Understanding master pages and layers" in online Help.

> ○ You can add an event name, logo, watermarked graphic or other object(s) to the master page if you would like them to appear on each 'ticket.'
>
> If you want to design a 'stub' for the ticket, add a second **Page Number** object to the master page.
>
> You might also design an area for a name and address to be written on the stub and ticket.

7   Click the **A ▾ Artistic Text** tool and then click in the top left of the publication and drag out a fairly large square to set a large font size for a new text object. When you release the mouse button and can see a flashing text-insertion cursor, click **Insert**, then **Page Number**.

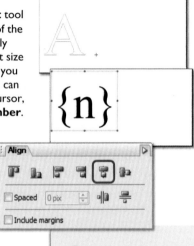

You'll see {n} or an actual page number on your page.

8   Select the **{n}**:

   • On the **Align** tab, click **Centre Horizontally**.

   • On the Text context toolbar, click the
     ☰ Align Centre button.

> ○ Using centred alignment means that as your page number extends from 1 to 2 to 3 characters, the entire number will remain centred.

9   Use the **╲ Straight Line** tool to add two short straight lines to the lower right corner of the page. We chose a light grey colour (RGB 203, 203, 203) from the **Swatches** tab. These will help you to score the tickets or trim the pages ready to use as a ticket book.

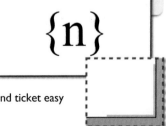

If you have designed a stub for the ticket, draw another line to score down after printing to make the stub and ticket easy to separate.

10 At the lower left of the workspace, click the Current Page box (currently displaying **Master A**) to switch back to normal page view.

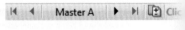

11 On the **Pages** tab, click the **Page Manager** button.

On the **Insert** tab, choose to insert 99 pages and click **OK**.

You now have a 100-page publication (printable on just 10 pieces of paper), with the publication automatically set at 10% of your chosen printer page size.

12 On the **File** menu, click **Print Preview**.

Congratulations, you now have the beginnings of a sequentially-numbered ticket book, using the paper size of your choice and automatically sized 'tickets' based simply on the number of rows and columns specified!

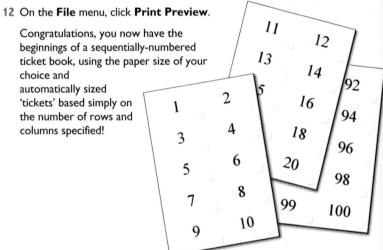

💡 Creating numbers with leading zeros

To prefix your automatic numbering with leading zeros, type them directly into the text frame in front of the page number field. You'll need to create a separate ticket book file for each 'set' of leading zeros required. For example, for tickets numbered 001 to 200, you'll need to create the following:

Numbers 1 to 9:

- Create a book of nine tickets. Prefix your page number with *two* leading zeros like this—00{n}.

Numbers 10 to 99:

- Create a book of 90 tickets. Prefix your page number with *one* leading zero like this—0{n}.

- Click **Format** then **Page Number Format** and change the first page number to 10.

Numbers 100 to 200:

- Create a book of 101 tickets. Insert a page number with *no* leading zeros—{n}.

- Click **Format** then **Page Number Format** and change the first page number to 100.

Creating Address Labels

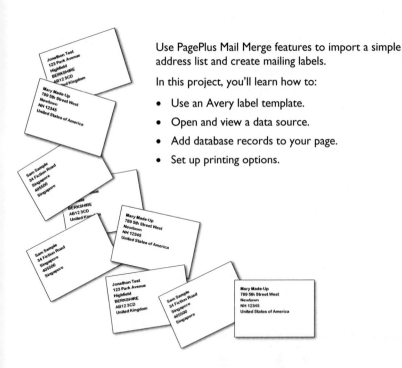

Use PagePlus Mail Merge features to import a simple address list and create mailing labels.

In this project, you'll learn how to:

- Use an Avery label template.
- Open and view a data source.
- Add database records to your page.
- Set up printing options.

Creating Address Labels

In PagePlus, **mail merge** means printing your publication a number of times, inserting different information each time from a data source—in this case an address list file—into a series of form letters or mailing labels.

1 From the Startup Wizard, choose **Start New Publication** and browse the **Small Publications > Avery > Address Labels** category of blank documents.

   Depending on whether you chose a US or European setup at the time of installation, you'll find either US or European label definitions due to the differing paper size standards.

PagePlus can handle many kinds of data sources and more challenging creative tasks. It's even possible to merge picture data into single fields or even auto-create a grid layout of pictures and text suitable for catalogues or photo albums (see the "Creating an Auction Catalogue" project).

2 Choose either **Parcel L7165** (based on A4 paper) or **Namebadge 5095** (based on Letter paper) and click **Open**. Your publication displays as a single label.

3 On the Tools toolbar, click the **Standard Text Frame** tool and create a text frame to cover the size of the page area contained within the blue guidelines—if you can't see the guidelines, click **View** then **Guidelines**.

4 On the **Tools** menu, point to **Mail and Photo Merge**, and then click **Open Data Source...**.

5 In the **Open** dialog, in the **Files of Type** list (highlighted in blue in our illustration) and select **Text Files (*.txt, *.csv, *.tab, *.asc)**.

> **testdata.csv** is a comma separated file—entries are delimited by commas—and was created using an address book from an email client program. Most address-management applications and database and spreadsheet programs can create such standard comma-separated files, which you can import.
>
> You can also take advantage of the **New Data Source** command to create your own editable databases in PagePlus.

Select the **testdata.csv** file found in your **...\Tutorials\Workspace** folder (normally located at:

C:\Program Files\Serif\PagePlus\X3) and click **Open**.

The process of importing your data will begin.

6   In the **Data Format** dialog:

   - Click **Delimited**, select **First Line Contains Column Headers**, and then click **Next**.

   - Select **Comma**, and then click **Finish**.

The **testdata.csv** file opens and is now your active **data source**. The **Merge List** dialog shows you the active data source and lets you further select, filter, or sort it for the impending merge operation.

For example, you could prevent certain records from being merged, either by clearing the boxes one by one or by applying a filter (for instance, where City is Not equal to Nottingham).

7   For now, simply click **OK** to include all the data in your merge list.

You should see the **Mail and Photo Merge** toolbar, indicating that there's an active data source.

8   On the **Mail and Photo Merge** toolbar, click the  **Insert Text Field** button.

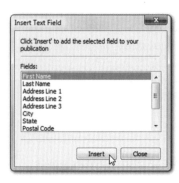

In the **Insert Mail Merge Text Field** dialog:

- Select **First Name**, click **Insert**, and then press the spacebar.

- Select **Last Name** and click **Insert**.

This inserts the **First Name** and **Last Name** data fields on the same line in your text frame with a space between them.

Now for the address.

9 Press the **Enter** key, select the **Address Line 1** field, click **Insert**, then press the **Enter** key again.

10 Repeat this process of selecting the field name, clicking **Insert**, and then pressing **Enter** until you have inserted each of the address fields on a line of its own in your text frame. Click **Close** when you've finished.

11 On the Frame context toolbar, click the ⊠ **AutoFit** button to force the text to fill the available frame area.

(You can reformat these fields in your text frame as if they were normal text, except that each field will be treated as a single character.)

All of the hard work is done! PagePlus has created the database from an external file and has set up a text frame to contain all of the mail merge data.

12 On the **Mail and Photo Merge** toolbar, click the ▤ **View Data** button. You can now use the arrow buttons on the toolbar (such as the ▶ **Next Record** button) to browse each of the database records in turn merged into your frame.

13 When you're happy to proceed, click the 🖨 **Print** button on the **Standard** toolbar.

14 In the **Print** dialog, click the **Layout** tab.

- In the **Multiple Pages per Sheet** section, on the drop-down menu, choose **Each page N times**. In the **N times** box, set the value to '1.'

- In the **Mail & Photo Merge** section, select the **All records** option.

- Click **Print**.

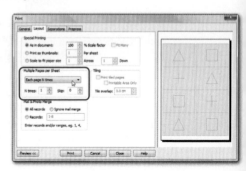

You should now have a printed page containing addresses formatted as if they were on the label you chose at the beginning of the project.

If your address database had consisted of more than eight records, the printed output would have continued on to subsequent pages.

For instructions on how to print on partially-used label sheets, and how to select which addresses to print, see the "Using mail merge" and "Printing special formats" online Help topics.

Congratulations on successfully creating a mail-merged publication! The same principles can be used to create tailored newsletters, photo-based catalogue layouts, and much more!

Creating an Auction Catalogue

In this project, you'll make use of the PagePlus Mail Merge functionality to merge both photos and text into an auction house catalogue.

We'll show you how to:

- Create a small database in PagePlus from a batch of photos.

- Annotate each photo with a caption.

- Design a repeating layout with a grid of 'listings,' where each listing includes a photo and its caption.

- Merge to a new publication that will display all the listings.

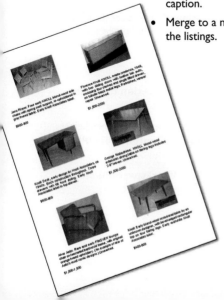

Creating an Auction Catalogue

In a traditional mail merge operation—for example, filling names and addresses into a batch of form letters or labels—you start with a data source such as a contact list or address book (see the "Creating Address Labels" project for an example).

This project demonstrates a different type of mail merge operation, using a simple comma-delimited (*.csv) file as the data source.

In this approach—ideal for a catalogue or photo album—you define a **repeating layout** with placeholder fields arranged in a grid.

> This project provides a 'hands-on' example, without a lot of additional comments. For more details, see related topics, "Using Advanced Document Features" in online Help.

You'll insert placeholder fields into your publication and specify which data field should map to each placeholder. Then you'll print the publication a number of times. With each successive printout, data from the next record is merged into the output.

During the merge, PagePlus populates the grid fields with photo and text data, generating as many new pages as needed to accommodate the data set.

You'll find the sample data in your **...\Tutorials\Workspace\Pieces** folder. In a standard installation, this is installed to the following location:

C:\Program Files\Serif\PagePlus\X3

Creating the data source

1. Click **File**, point to **New**, then click **New Publication** to create a new, single-page publication using default settings.

2. On the **Tools** menu, click **Mail and Photo Merge**, and then select **Create Photo Data Source from Folder Contents**. The **Photo Data Source Wizard** opens.

3. Click the **Browse** button and locate the ...**Workspace\Pieces** folder. Select the folder, click **OK**, and then click **Next**.

4 Specify the file name for the database file to be created. We suggest you use the default filename provided (**Pieces.sdb**). Click **Next**.

The Wizard should list six image files located in the specified folder. Make sure they're all selected, and then click **Next**.

5 On the following screen, click **Select None** to clear all the **Summary Item** check boxes (these refer to digital camera EXIF information, which you might want for original snapshots but not in this case). Now click **Finish**.

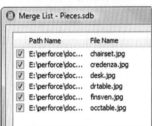

PagePlus creates a small Serif Database (SDB) file and displays its records in the **Merge List** dialog.

The SDB format is the same as that used to store address list data for traditional mail merge, but in this case it consists of six records (one for each image), with three fields for each record: **File Name**, **Path Name**, and **Date Modified**.

> The **Merge List** dialog lets you filter, sort, or otherwise pare down the full SDB data set for the next merge operation. When you finally merge, only the items displayed and checked in your merge list will actually be merged.

The SDB file stores the full data and will be recorded as the active data source when you save this publication.

Adding caption data

An advantage of having the photos listed in an SDB database is that you can edit the accompanying data and PagePlus can save changes as part of the SDB file. Let's add some caption data to our mini image database.

1 In the **Merge List** dialog, click the **Edit** button.

2 The **Edit Database** dialog opens, displaying data for the first record. From here, you can browse the records or use **Add** and **Delete** to expand or reduce the data set.

3 Click the **Customize** button. The **Customize Database** dialog displays the three fields.

Click **Insert**.

4 In the **Field Name** dialog, type "Description" as the new field name, then click **OK**.

5 Click the **Move Down** button if necessary to place the field at the bottom of the list.

6 Click **Insert** again, type "Appraisal," and then click **OK**. Again, move the field to the bottom of the list and then click **OK**.

Now we've got two new fields available in the database. The next step is some basic data entry.

7 In Windows Explorer, browse to your **Workspace** folder and open the **AuctionData.rtf** file.

As an RTF (Rich Text Format) file, by default it should open in a word processor or text editing program.

8 Use copy and paste to transfer the information to your database.

In the **View Records** section of the dialog, click the arrow buttons to step through the records.

9 When you've finished, click **OK** to save changes to the data source. In the **Merge List** dialog, you'll see the data you entered displayed in two new columns.

There are various ways to fine-tune the repeating area—read all about them in online Help.

10 Click **OK** to close the **Merge List** dialog (the current merge list data remains active for the next merge operation). You'll see that the **Mail and Photo Merge** toolbar has opened to assist you with your next steps.

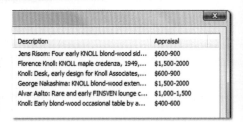

Description	Appraisal
Jens Risom: Four early KNOLL blond-wood sid...	$600-900
Florence Knoll: KNOLL maple credenza, 1949,...	$1,500-2000
Knoll: Desk, early design for Knoll Associates,...	$600-900
George Nakashima: KNOLL blond-wood exten...	$1,500-2000
Alvar Aalto: Rare and early FINSVEN lounge c...	$1,000-1,500
Knoll: Early blond-wood occasional table by a...	$400-600

Designing a repeating layout

To produce a repeating layout in a new publication, you need to specify a **repeating area** in the original document—basically a single cell whose unit size determines how many can be tiled across and down on a page.

Within this repeating area, you can put placeholders—picture fields or text fields where you want merged data to appear—and other design elements such as artistic text or QuickShapes. At merge time, data from one record at a time will get merged into each cell of the resulting grid. You'll see how this works in a moment.

1 On the Mail and Photo Merge toolbar, click the ⊞ **Create or Modify Repeating Area** button.

2 The **Repeating Area Tile Setup** dialog shows a page layout that consists of a 1 x 4 tiling grid: one repeating area across the page and four down. We have 6 images, so a 2 x 3 grid makes more sense.

3 In the **Tile Setup** dialog:

   - In the **Layout** section, enter an **Across** value of **2** and a **Down** value of **3**.

   - In the **Size** section, use the arrow buttons to increase the **Height** of the repeating area until the 2 x 3 grid occupies nearly all of the page area. When your preview region in the

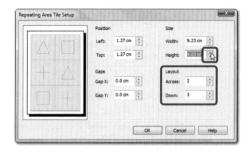

left of the dialog looks like our example, click **OK**.

The repeating area appears as a single cell at the upper left of your blank page. Its inner text confirms that we can fit "2 across by 3 down" of these cells on the current page.

4 If you haven't saved your publication yet, do it now.

5 On the Mail and Photo Merge toolbar, click the  **Insert Picture Field** button.

The dialog lists available picture fields in the current data source—in this case there's just one, 'Path Name.'

- Click **Insert** once; the dialog stays open in case you want to insert more than one field.

- Click **Close**. A new picture field appears on the page (ensure you've added only one).

6 Drag the picture field into the repeating area and make sure it's entirely within the area. It will turn light grey to let you know it fits within the cell. Resize the field and position it as shown. Select both objects and use the **Align** tab to **Centre Horizontally**.

On the Picture context toolbar, click **Frame Properties**. Click **Scale to Minimum Fit** and click **OK**.

If you select the repeating area at this point and move it slightly, you'll see that the picture field moves along with it. PagePlus treats any object fully inside a repeating area as part of the area. Be sure to undo the move operation.

7 Now click the **Insert Text Field** button on the Mail and Photo Merge toolbar. This time, insert two fields—**Description** and **Appraisal**. Close the dialog and you'll see a text frame containing two text fields.

8 Drag the text frame into position below the picture field. Between the two text fields, press the **Enter** key twice to place the **Appraisal** field on a separate line.

9 Select the text frame and change the font to 11 pt Arial using the Text context toolbar.

10 Before proceeding, check the dimensions displayed in the upper left and lower right corners of the repeating area to ensure that your layout is still set up for a 2 x 3 grid.

11 Confirm that your picture and text fields are within the repeat area and then save the publication again.

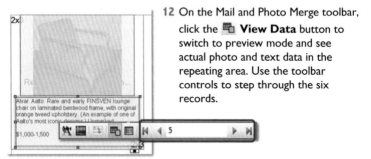

12 On the Mail and Photo Merge toolbar, click the **View Data** button to switch to preview mode and see actual photo and text data in the repeating area. Use the toolbar controls to step through the six records.

Merging to a new publication

On the **Tools** menu, click **Mail and Photo Merge > Merge Repeating Area to New Publication**.

PagePlus generates a new publication in a separate window, replicating the repeating area as many times as there are records (six in this case) and inserting new data into each region.

That's all there is to it! We'll leave you to experiment and consider the following additional pointers:

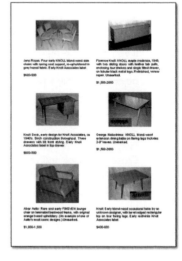

• The new publication is not yet saved. If you think you can improve on the layout, close its window without saving, make changes in the original publication and merge again.

• You can merge and save the results as many times as you like, using different file names. In fact, one of the advantages of repeating areas is that you only need to design your 'source' publication once—you can then reuse it with different data sources.

- The new publication no longer contains any repeating areas, picture fields, or text fields. Everything on the page is a 'regular' PagePlus object. This is useful because each

  > ⏻ Had our data source included more than six records, additional pages would have been created.

  publication supports a *maximum of one repeating area*. In a situation where you need more than one, you could produce the publication in stages—merge from the first repeat area, then create the second one in the new publication, merge again, etc.

- The merged photos sit inside **picture frames**, which work much like text frames—you can replace or edit their contents, whilst leaving the frame intact. To adjust display properties such as picture size and alignment for any individual picture frame, right-click it and choose **Properties > Frame Properties**.

We hope this exercise has cleared up any mysteries surrounding repeating areas and illustrated a novel use for traditional mail merge. For further information, see the relevant topics in online Help.

Design Lab

Our Design Lab offers a wealth of information for PagePlus users of all abilities. Whether you're creating a simple greeting card, a multi-page brochure, or a business Web site, we'll show you how to create effective, eye-catching layouts, choose the right colours for your publication, and make the most of your images and photographs. The focus here is on good desktop publishing techniques and practices to help you get the best out of your software.

To access files needed by the Lab exercises, browse to the **...\Tutorials\Workspace** folder in your PagePlus installation directory. In a standard installation, you'll find this in the following location:

C:\Program Files\Serif\PagePlus\X3

PagePlus Design Lab

Designing on a Grid

In this tutorial, we'll explore the design phase of document creation. With the grid as our layout guide, we'll look at the various ways that elements—text, images, graphic objects, and so on—can work together to produce effective layouts.

The grid provides a structured framework for a layout but it should not limit design or stifle creativity. Rather than forcing you to work rigidly within its confines, the grid layout should work for you, allowing you to dictate the look and feel of your publication. We're confident you'll never look back!

In the following pages, we'll discuss:

- Basic grid structures
- Asymmetrical grids
- Margins and row and column gaps
- Mixed grids
- Breaking out of the grid
- Choosing the right grid for your publication

Designing on a Grid

Grid structures are vital to successful document design, and especially so for documents containing a mixture of text and graphics. If you don't believe us, examine a few of those magazines in your doctor's waiting room. Whatever the subject matter, and no matter how random the layout appears, the underlying structure will generally be based on a carefully designed grid.

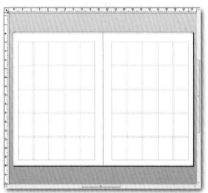

In the following pages, we'll look at some different grid structures and illustrate various layout options for each. Along the way, we'll offer tips and suggestions for creating successful grid-based layouts—we'll even encourage you to break the rules occasionally!

At the end of the tutorial, we'll provide some guidelines to help you choose the right grid for your particular project.

I: Basic grid structures

Let's start by looking at some basic grid structures.

Two-column grids

Two-column grids are mostly used in books, newsletters, or narrow publications where the column width is limited. Although this layout is very simple, you can still achieve variety by allowing some elements—for example, images, headlines, and so on—to span both columns on the page.

However, in wide publications, such as magazines or 'coffee table books,' the text columns in a two-column grid would generally be too wide for comfortable reading.

Three-column grids

These offer more flexibility than two-column grids because text and images can span one, two, or all of the columns. Three-column grids work for most layouts, even wide ones, and are particularly suited to publications that do not require complex arrangement of elements.

An alternative to the three-column grid is the three-row grid. This format is great for laying out narrow documents such as the tri-fold brochure.

Four- or more column grids

If you need to place a variety of elements into your layout—text, images, graphics, and so on—you'll find that grids with four or more columns offer the most flexibility.

Generally, grids with an uneven number of grid columns work best. Five- and even seven-column grids provide maximum flexibility and also allow for asymmetrical placement of elements, which tends to be more visually appealing than a symmetrical layout.

The examples on the right illustrate two different ways we can place the same information onto a seven-column grid.

Notice how we have created 'white space' by leaving some columns empty. Effective use of white space creates 'breathing space,' especially on a busy page.

⬛ 4-column grids can be problematic because a single column is often too narrow for comfortable reading or for placing a graphic. Unless you are sure this structure will work for you, you could end up with most layout elements spanning two columns. In this case, the finished layout will appear to be based on two columns rather than four.

2: Asymmetrical grids

One of the most important features of the grid structure is its flexibility. So far, we've shown you how to add interest to your pages by leaving a column empty. In this section, we'll explore this idea further and show you how asymmetrical grids can liven up your layouts.

⬛ For instructions on setting up asymmetrical grids, see the "Creating Grid Layouts" tutorial.

Basic three-column grid

Our first example—a basic grid consisting of three equally sized columns—displays text columns and images in a pleasing, but conventional arrangement. Note that some elements span multiple columns.

Basic three-column grid

Image spanning three columns

Image spanning two columns

Text frame spanning two columns

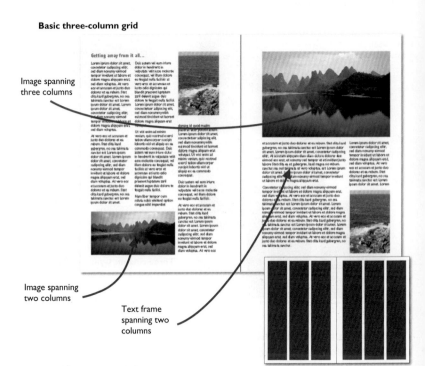

Three-column asymmetrical grid

In this example, we've dragged our column guides to make three columns of distinctly different sizes. To provide page-to-page consistency throughout our publication, we've created a 'mirrored' layout. Notice again that some elements span multiple columns, and that on the right page we have intentionally left the narrow centre column blank.

Narrow column used for pull quotes, or left blank to create white space.

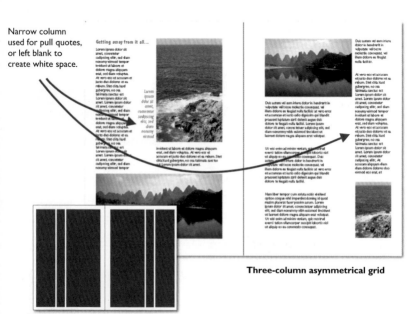

Three-column asymmetrical grid

Asymmetrical grid with sidebar

Our final example, illustrated on the following page, is a very popular asymmetrical layout. This grid makes use of a narrow side column, or 'sidebar,' which is not used for main body copy, but instead holds related text (headings, pull quotes, notes, and so on), graphics, or simply white space.

The following list describes some common uses of the sidebar:

* To display headings.

  Particularly useful in
  complex hierarchical
  documents, headings
  displayed in sidebar
  columns help to organize a
  document and allow the
  reader to quickly scan the
  page to find the
  information they are
  looking for.

* To bring the reader's
  attention to important
  information that you want to emphasize.

* To hold information that is relevant to the
  main subject of the body copy, but not part of
  the main text flow. For example, a note,
  suggestion, or warning.

* To 'declutter' a complex layout by providing
  white space.

On the left page of our sample layout, below, the sidebar holds an initial
adjacent cap and a note box. On the right page, the column is intentionally
left blank; this balances the spread and creates an open and airy feel that
complements the imagery perfectly.

Asymmetrical grid with sidebar

This example uses the same grid structure to create a very different look and feel.

Here, a single text column is flanked by a narrow sidebar and an image. The ample white space allows the images to dominate the page.

3: Margins and row and column gaps

Besides choosing the number, width, and arrangement of your columns, there are some other important grid elements that you must consider: page margins and row and column gaps.

Page margins

No matter what type of document you're working on, it's rare that your page margins will all be of equal width. For example, you may want more space at the top or bottom of each page—for page header or page footer information, page numbers, and so on.

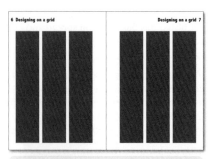

For bound publications, you'll usually find that the inside margins are considerably wider than the outside margins. This prevents text and images that are placed in the centre of a spread from 'disappearing' into the spine.

If your document is to be printed professionally, avoid last-minute problems by discussing margins and gutter widths with your printer—*before* you start creating your layout.

Row and column gaps

Row and column gaps are the spaces between the rows and columns in a grid structure.

There are no strict rules about the width of these spaces, but if you make them too narrow your text columns will be difficult to read. We suggest that you experiment to find the gap width that works best for your particular layout.

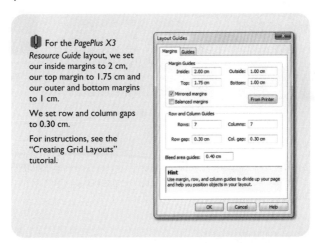

For the *PagePlus X3 Resource Guide* layout, we set our inside margins to 2 cm, our top margin to 1.75 cm and our outer and bottom margins to 1 cm.

We set row and column gaps to 0.30 cm.

For instructions, see the "Creating Grid Layouts" tutorial.

4: Mixed grid layouts

We've stressed the importance of using a grid to maintain page-to-page consistency throughout a document. However, if certain pages present information that varies greatly from the rest of the document, don't try to force them to conform to a structure that doesn't really suit the purpose. Instead, simply use a different grid for these pages.

Let's suppose we're creating a brochure that contains lots of text, and some images that we want to present all together on one or two pages. For this project, it makes sense to use one grid for the text-heavy pages and another for displaying the images.

In our example, the main pages are based on an asymmetrical three-column grid—two wide columns for the main text flow and a narrow sidebar for headings, pull quotes and selected images. Pages displaying images only are based on a basic 3 x 3 grid.

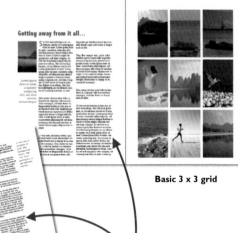

Basic 3 x 3 grid

3-column asymmetrical grid

5: Breaking out of the grid

We've convinced you (we hope!) of the power and flexibility of the grid. Now, we'll encourage you to break the rules and occasionally break out of the grid.

Example I

Add impact and visual interest to a layout by extending an element out to the page edge.

This works especially well for presenting large images (we've used this technique in this tutorial!).

Example 2

Try positioning some elements outside of the grid. On the right page of the newsletter spread below, see how the text frame containing the pull quote is centred on the page, breaking the underlying three-column grid structure.

Example 3

If you're feeling adventurous, why not break the grid by rotating some layout objects. Be careful not to overdo this one though, and make sure that other elements remain within the grid, or your page will appear disorganized.

Example 4

Diagonal lines can add interest to a grid layout. In this example, we've cut through our columns, but have still aligned the image with the grid.

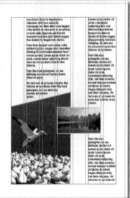

6: Choosing the right grid

When planning your layout, you need to have a clear idea of what your finished document should look like, what format is required, the purpose of the document, who will be reading it, how it will be printed, and so on. Once you've answered these questions, you'll have a better understanding of the type of grid structure required. The following guidelines should help you choose and plan your grid layout.

Content

The most important question to ask yourself is this: "Is the document predominantly text or images?" For lots of text with few images, try a simple one-, two- or three-column grid.

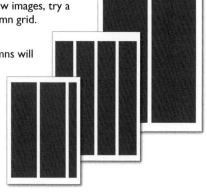

For lots of graphics, photos, or illustrations, four or more columns will give you more scope to place and size these elements.

Do you want to include notes, pull quotes, or other accent information? Is the document hierarchical, with lots of headings and subheadings? If so, consider an asymmetrical grid with a sidebar column.

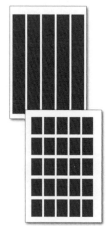

Complexity

For complex documents—for example, a newsletter containing a mix of text and graphics—grids with more columns and/or rows provide more design options. However, avoid making the grid too complex or you'll lose sight of the underlying structure.

Document type

Newsletters usually contain more text so simple column-based layouts tend to work best. For more sophisticated publications, such as illustrated books, more columns will provide more design options. Publications with mainly small articles and graphics—a sales brochure or catalogue, for example—are more suited to grids containing both columns and rows.

Summary

In this tutorial, our main objective was to illustrate the power and flexibility of the grid, and explain why it is such an important document design tool. We hope that we've achieved this objective.

To quickly get started with grids, you'll find some sample layouts in the **..\Tutorials\Workspace\Grid Layouts** folder of your PagePlus installation directory. For step-by-step instructions on setting up a grid structure from scratch, see the "Creating Grid Layouts" tutorial.

Q Design tips

- Don't confine page elements to individual grid units. In grids with four or more columns, text and images can span several grid units.

- Leave some grid units empty, or use them for accents such as small photos, adjacent caps, headlines, and so on.

- Use your gutters and margins. Extending some images and headlines into the 'bleed area' can add interest to a layout.

Creating Grid Layouts

Effective document design depends on a clear visual structure that conveys and complements the main message. The right layout should provide a consistent framework to help you organize the various elements of your pages, but should also be flexible enough to let you exercise your creativity.

In the previous tutorial, "Designing on a Grid," we explored the various ways that layout elements can be placed together on an underlying invisible grid structure.

In this tutorial, we will continue with this theme and show you how to set up a basic grid for a multi-column layout.

You'll learn how to:

- Use the Page Setup dialog to set up your page size and type.
- Use the Layout Guides dialog to set up margins, columns, rows, and bleed area guides.
- Work with ruler guides.
- Create asymmetrical grids.
- View and customize the dot grid.

Creating Grid Layouts

The grid is a traditional layout tool that dates back to the days when text was typeset onto vertical strips of paper, which were then manually cut and pasted onto card sheets. The print production process has changed dramatically since then, but the grid is still a popular page layout tool because it provides some crucial functions—for both reader and designer.

When reading any type of document, we expect a certain consistency from page to page. For example, we expect to find page numbers, footnotes, sidebar text, and so on, in the same place on each page. When all the text and design elements in a document have a consistent look and feel, readability is significantly enhanced.

A grid structure—such as the one illustrated here (used for this document)—makes it easier to provide this consistency by helping to determine such things as the width of text columns, the space around images and graphic objects, the placement of repeating elements throughout a publication, and so on. As you work with the grid, you'll find that having these guidelines for object placement significantly speeds up the layout process, and helps to ensure that your final layout will be a success.

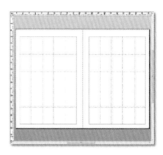

In this tutorial, we'll introduce you to the various elements of the grid, and show you how to set up a basic grid structure in PagePlus.

Using grid templates

If you want to use a grid, but don't want to create one from scratch, you can quickly get started with one of our ready-made grid templates. In a standard installation, you'll find these in the

...\Tutorials\Workspace\Grid Layouts folder in the following location:

C:\Program Files\Serif\PagePlus\X3

You can use the templates 'as is,' or customize them to suit your needs using the procedures outlined in the following sections.

1: Setting up the page

Our first task is to create a new document and set up our page size and type.

To set up the page

1   On the **File** menu, select **New**, then click **New from Startup Wizard**.

    In the Startup Wizard, click **start from scratch**, choose **A4** or **Letter** size paper, and click **OK**.

    Let's add two pages to this publication.

2   In the Hintline toolbar, click the  **Page Manager** (or click **Insert**, then **Page**).

3   In the **Page Manager** dialog, on the **Insert** tab:

- In the **Number of pages** box, type **2**.

  Notice that we can also select *where* to add our pages. For example, if this were a multi-page document, we could select **Before** or **After**, and then choose the page number from the drop-down list.

- We just have one page, so accept the default values (**After, Page 1**). Click **OK**.

The Hintline toolbar now displays '2 of 3,' indicating that you are currently working on page 2 of a 3 page document.

4   On the **File** menu, click **Page Setup**. In the **Page Setup** dialog:

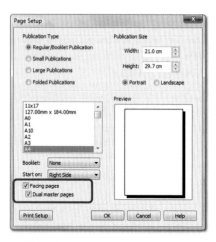

*   To set up the page layout as facing pages (also known as spreads), select the **Facing pages** check box.

*   To set up dual master pages (allowing you to run elements across the spread in the background of the publication, or position left- and right-side page numbers), select the **Dual master pages** check box.

*   Click **OK**.

If you're setting up a facing-page layout where both left and right pages share the same master page, and you don't need to run background elements across the spread, clear the **Dual master pages check** box.

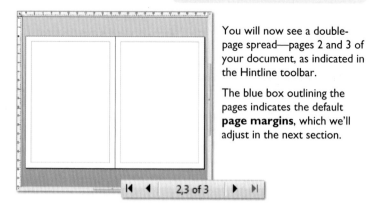

You will now see a double-page spread—pages 2 and 3 of your document, as indicated in the Hintline toolbar.

The blue box outlining the pages indicates the default **page margins**, which we'll adjust in the next section.

2: Setting up layout guides

Layout guides are visual guide lines that help you position layout elements, either 'by eye' or with snapping turned on (you'll find the ⊞ **Snapping** button at the right of the Hintline toolbar). Layout guides include page margins, row and column guides, and bleed area guides. In PagePlus, margins are shown as solid blue lines; row, column, and bleed area guides are shown as dashed blue lines.

To set up layout guides

1   Click on a blank area of the page and then on the Page context toolbar, click ⊞ Layout Guides . (You can also click **File**, then **Layout Guides**, or right-click on a blank area of the page and choose **Layout Guides**.)

In the **Layout Guides** dialog, in the **Margin Guides** section:

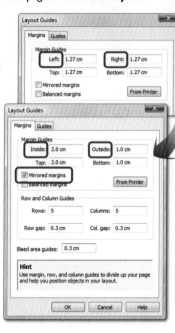

- Select the **Mirrored margins** check box.

    This tells PagePlus to change the **Left** margin setting to the '**Inside**' margin on both facing pages, and to change the **Right** margin to the '**Outside**' margin on both pages.

- Set the **Inside page margin to** **2.00** cm.

- Set the **Outside page margin** to **1.00** cm.

- Set the **Top page** margin to **2.00** cm.

- Set the **Bottom page** margin to **1.00** cm.

2   In the **Row and Column Guides** section:

- Set the number of **Rows to 5**.

- Set the number of **Columns to 5**.

- Set the **Row gap** (the space between your rows) to **0.30** cm.

- Set the **Column gap** (the space between your columns) to **0.30** cm.

- Set the **Bleed area guides** (the 'trim edge' of the page) to **0.30** cm.

3 Click **OK**.

You should now see a 5 x 5 blue grid superimposed on each of your pages. Note also that the position of the margins has changed.

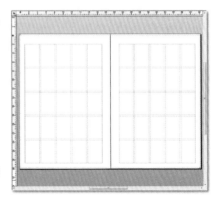

Can't see your layout guides? On the **View** menu, ensure that **Guide Lines** and **Bleed Area Guides** are selected.

Bleed area guides

These guides help you to position 'bleed elements' that you want to run to the edge of a page. If your document is to be professionally printed, we suggest that you allow for inaccuracies in the trimming process by extending any bleed elements beyond the trim edge.

The page border expands by the distance specified, and the trim edge is shown with dashed lines and 'scissors' symbols.

Note that these guide lines are *visual aids* only; the **Print** dialog's **Bleed limit** setting extends the *actual* output page size.

See "Setting prepress options" in the "Generating professional output" online Help topic.

3: Adding ruler guides

You can set up horizontal and vertical 'snap-to' ruler guides—non-printing, solid red lines that you can use to align headlines, pictures, and other layout elements.

There are two ways to create ruler guides:

- Automatically—in the **Layout Guides** dialog, on the **Guides** tab. Use this method to place multiple ruler guides onto a page in precise positions.

- or -

- Manually—by clicking and dragging on the rulers. Use this method to place individual ruler guides onto a page as you work.

To create a ruler guide automatically

1 Click on a blank area of the page and then on the Page context bar, click 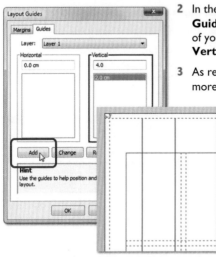 Layout Guides .

2 In the **Layout Guides** dialog, on the **Guides** tab, type the desired position of your guide into the **Horizontal** or **Vertical** box. Click **Add**.

3 As required, repeat step 2 to add more guides, and then click **OK**.

Solid red lines now indicate the ruler guides you created.

To create a guide manually

• Click and drag on the horizontal or vertical ruler.

A red line indicates the new ruler guide.

If you now open the **Layout Guides** dialog and view the **Guides** tab, you'll see that your guide has been added to the list.

The dialog on the right shows the guides we created to position the page headers and numbers in our publication.

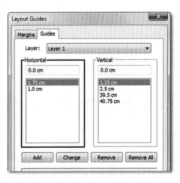

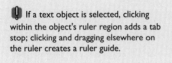

 If a text object is selected, clicking within the object's ruler region adds a tab stop; clicking and dragging elsewhere on the ruler creates a ruler guide.

Moving and deleting ruler guides

Whichever method you use to create your ruler guides, you can move them around or delete them at any time.

To move a ruler guide

- Click and drag the red guide line.

  As you drag, the solid line changes to a dashed line; once positioned, the line again becomes solid.

To delete a ruler guide

- In the **Layout Guides** dialog: On the **Guides** tab, select the guide and click **Remove** (to delete all ruler guides, click **Remove All**.)

- or -

- On the page: Drag and drop the red guide line anywhere outside the page area.

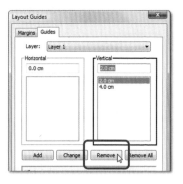

💡 **Locking and resetting your guide lines**

To prevent your margins, columns, rows, and ruler guides from accidentally being moved, you can lock them.

To lock your guides:

1 On the **Tools** menu, click **Options**.

2 In the left **Options** list, select **Layout**.

3 Select the **Lock guide lines** check box and click **OK**.

Note that this option will also lock the red ruler guides, so you will not be able to drag them freely around your page.

If you choose not to lock your guidelines, you can still easily reset your original layout.

To reset your layout

- Click **File > Layout Guides**, click the **Margins** tab, and then click **OK**.

4: Creating asymmetrical grids

Once you've set up your basic row and column guides, you can manually adjust them to make your layouts even more flexible. This feature is particularly useful for setting up asymmetrical grid layouts, such as the three-column layout illustrated here.

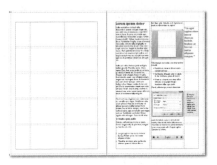

(In order to move the row and column guides, you must clear the **Lock guide lines** option in the **Options** dialog.)

To adjust custom rows and columns

• Click and drag a dashed blue row or column guide line.

You will have to adjust the row and column guides on each page of your document.

5: Asymmetrical grids on multi-page documents

When working on multi-page documents, rather than manually adjusting the row and column guides on each page of your document, there are various ways to speed up the process.

Note: For each of the following methods, you'll first need to make sure that the **Facing pages** and **Dual master pages** options are selected in the **Page Setup** dialog.

Asymmetrical grid: Method 1

1   In **Normal** page view, open the **Layout Guides** dialog.

On the **Margins** tab, set up the basic number of grid units for your publication.

2 In **Master Page** view, add ruler guides to mark the asymmetrical units. You can set these up manually or automatically, as you prefer (see section 3, "Adding ruler guides").

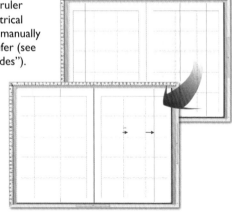

These guides will be visible on all pages of the publication.

3 In **Normal** page view, drag the row and column guides onto the ruler guides as you work on each page. You'll need to zoom in quite a lot to achieve precise guide placement. As the guides line up exactly, you may find that your ruler guide disappears underneath the layout guide.

Asymmetrical grid: Method 2

1 In **Normal** page view, open the **Layout Guides** dialog. On the **Margins** tab, set up a basic grid comprising a few more grid units than you need.

For example, to end up with a three-column asymmetrical grid, try starting with a basic five- or six-column grid.

In our illustration we used a basic seven-column grid as the starting point for a four-column asymmetrical layout.

You may need to experiment with this to get it right.

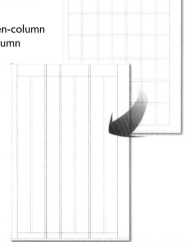

2 In **Master Page** view, use ruler guides to mark the asymmetrical grid units. You can set these up manually or automatically, as you prefer (see section 3, "Adding ruler guides").

These guides will be visible on all pages of the publication.

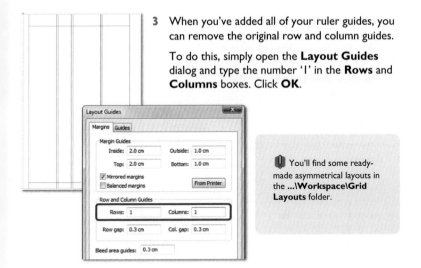

3 When you've added all of your ruler guides, you can remove the original row and column guides.

To do this, simply open the **Layout Guides** dialog and type the number '1' in the **Rows** and **Columns** boxes. Click **OK**.

> 💡 You'll find some ready-made asymmetrical layouts in the **...\Workspace\Grid Layouts** folder.

Asymmetrical grid: Method 3

1 In **Normal** page view, in the **Layout Guides** dialog, set up a one row, one column grid.

2 In **Master Page** view, set up your asymmetrical grid using only the red ruler guides. You can set these up manually or automatically, as you prefer (see section 3, "Adding ruler guides").

These guides will be visible on all pages of the publication.

6: Using the dot grid

PagePlus provides an optional dot grid, which you can use for precise placement of layout elements. If required, you can customize the dot grid—for example, by changing the grid display type and colour.

To display or hide the dot grid

- On the **View** menu, click **Dot Grid**.

To customize the dot grid

1   On the **Tools** menu, click **Options**.

2   In the left **Options** list, select **Snapping**.

3   Select the **Dot Grid** check box.

Subdivisions

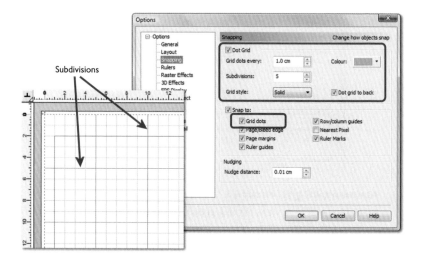

4   Make the following changes as required:

- In the **Grid dots every** box, choose the dot grid spacing.

- To highlight certain lines, set the **Subdivisions**. In our example, every fifth line is highlighted.

- In the **Grid style** drop-down list, choose the grid display type.

  For example, to create the graph-paper effect shown here, choose **Solid**.

- In the **Colour** box, click to select a new grid colour from the drop-down palette. If you are using subdivisions, mid to light greys produce the clearest display.

- If you want your layout elements to snap to the dot grid, in the **Snap to** section, select the **Grid dots** option.

- Check the **Dot grid to back** option if you want the grid to appear behind the objects on the page.

What's next?

If you've followed the steps of this tutorial, you should now know how to set up a grid layout for any type of publication.

When you are happy with your layout, you can start placing your text and graphics elements onto it. If you need help with this, refer back to the previous tutorial, "Designing on a Grid," for some layout ideas.

Creative Cropping

Whether you're using PagePlus to create a newsletter, brochure, Web site, or even a simple greeting card, chances are that at some point you'll be working with images.

In this tutorial, we'll show you how effective image cropping can improve a layout by creating a focal point, emphasizing a concept, removing unwanted elements, or simply adding drama to your pages.

You'll learn how to:

- Apply the Rule of Thirds.
- Make small spaces work for you.
- Use zoom and 'extreme cropping' techniques.
- Make the most of the white space on your page.
- Isolate sections of an image to create variety.
- Crop away the boring bits!

Creative Cropping

You may have found the perfect photo for your paper publication or your Web site, but that doesn't mean that you can't improve it. Every image has boundaries, and you can decide where those boundaries should be. In the following pages, we'll illustrate some effective and powerful cropping techniques that are sure to improve your layouts. Try them with your own photos—you'll be surprised what a difference they can make.

1: Apply the Rule of Thirds

The photographer's favourite, this rule states that if you divide your image roughly into thirds, horizontally and vertically, any point(s) where those lines intersect is a good place to position your main subject. Your chosen image may not conform to this standard, but you can correct this with some creative cropping.

For example, we've cropped this image so that our subject is positioned roughly at the one-third point. We've focused in on the runner and kept enough of the background to provide context.

Notice also that although we have cropped away the lower and upper portions of the subject, we have still maintained the essence of the image.

2: Make the most of small spaces

Small layouts can be problematic, and especially when you want to include an image. Many people make the mistake of simply resizing their image to fit into the space, which usually reduces the impact and results in a weak composition. Instead, crop your image effectively and make that small space work for you! Let's look at two common 'small space' design challenges: Web banners and business cards.

Web site banner

Here, the challenge lay in conveying the message of the site in a very shallow space.

To solve the problem, we looked for a photo that we could 'slice,' while still presenting enough information to get the message across.

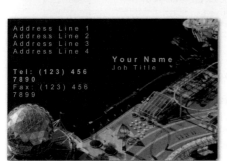

Business card

Here, you might be tempted to use the whole image, simply resizing it to fit the dimensions of the business card.

However, by zooming into a section of the image, we've given our design much more impact and have opened up a space to position our text elements.

3: Zoom in

Zooming closely into a subject and then using extreme cropping can strengthen a focal point and add to the drama in an image.

In our first example, we zoomed in closely and cropped away everything but the subjects. By doing so, we heightened the drama in an already dynamic image.

You can use this technique on many different types of images, but it's especially effective for portraits. When cropping portrait photos, aim to crop at eye-level, which is about two-fifths of the way down the page.

Note that as you zoom and crop closer and closer to your subject, you increase the drama and emotion conveyed in the image.

4: Isolate sections of an image

Isolating different sections of an image or images can be a great way to create variety and add 'movement' to your page. You can also use this technique to convey different stories from the same image.

Wedding album

In this example, we've contrasted a single vertical slice with a rectangular crop of the wedding bouquet.

In this example, we cropped vertical slices from three photos to create an interesting wedding album cover.

This composition works particularly well because the three images share similar coloration.

Slicing the images into narrow columns creates movement and moves the eye down the page.

Our wedding

Using white space

In both examples, notice how we have made use of white space by reducing the size of our composition relative to the page. This effectively 'disconnects' the image from the page edge so it appears to be borderless.

In the first example, rather than centring the subject vertically on the page, we have raised it to give three different margin widths. This again helps to eliminate the border effect.

Flyer

Here, we've cropped sections from the same image to create an interesting montage effect for a coffee shop flyer.

For the solid blocks of colour and the text, we used the

✎ **Colour Picker** tool (on the **Colour** tab) to sample colours directly from our image.

To learn more about this technique, see the "Working With Colour Schemes" tutorial.

The same effect would work equally well on a Web site or brochure, or even as the cover of family photo album...

💡 Using different zoom levels creates contrast and variety, adding interest to the page.

5: Crop away the boring bits!

We couldn't end this tutorial without stressing the most important cropping tip: get rid of the boring stuff!

Unless you're a professional photographer, you'll usually find that even your best planned photos contain elements that you don't want. Be strict with yourself and crop away anything that doesn't contribute to the image—we guarantee you'll be much happier with the results.

Working With Colour Schemes

When designing your publications, one of the most important factors to consider is colour. Choose wisely and you'll attract the attention of your target audience, set the appropriate mood, and send the right message. Choose unwisely and you'll turn readers away—no matter how professional your layout or how interesting your content.

But how do you select a colour palette that's right for your publication? In this tutorial, we'll demystify the process and show you a few different ways to find the perfect colour for your projects. Along the way, we'll introduce you to the predesigned PagePlus colour schemes, which you can apply to any design element.

You'll learn how to:

- Apply a preset colour scheme from the Scheme Manager.
- Modify an existing colour scheme.
- Create your own colour scheme from scratch.
- Create a colour scheme from a photograph.
- Use colour theory to create a range of palettes.

Working With Colour Schemes

In the first section of this tutorial, we'll apply scheme colours to individual elements on a page. We'll then show you how you can edit and modify scheme colours. Finally, we'll create a custom colour scheme from scratch. Let's get started...

Applying scheme colours to objects

You can apply a colour scheme at any point during the design process. Each publication can have just one colour scheme at a time and can easily switch from one to another.

To apply a colour scheme

1 Click **File**, then **Open**—or from the PagePlus Startup Wizard, select **Open Saved Publication**.

   Browse to the **...\Tutorials\Workspace\Colour Schemes** folder and open the **Health.ppp** file. In a standard installation, you'll find this file in the following location:

   C:\Program Files\Serif\PagePlus\X3

2 Click the **Schemes** tab.

   You'll see an assortment of named schemes, each consisting of five basic colours.

   The colour scheme that is currently applied throughout this publication is highlighted.

3 Right-click on the **Schemes** tab and select **Scheme Manager** (or click **Tools**, then **Scheme Manager**).

   In the **Scheme Manager** dialog, click the **Schemes** tab.

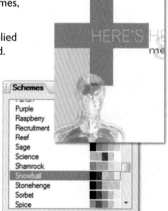

4 Click a few different colour schemes.

As you select each new scheme, watch the **Preview** pane—you'll see various elements on the page change colour.

So what exactly is happening here?

The scheme colours work much like a paint-by-numbers system, where various regions and elements of a page layout are coded with numbers. In each scheme, a specific colour is assigned to each number.

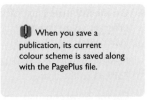

When you save a publication, its current colour scheme is saved along with the PagePlus file.

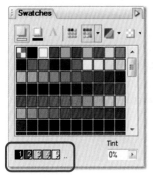

When you switch to a different scheme, any elements in the publication that have been assigned one of the scheme colour numbers are updated with the corresponding colour from the new scheme.

Let's see this in action...

5 On the Tools toolbar, on the **QuickShape** flyout, click the ☐ **Quick Rectangle** and draw a large shape on the page.

6 Click to display the **Swatches** tab.

At the bottom of the tab, below the colour swatches, you'll see that the five main colours of the current colour scheme appear as numbered swatches.

7 Select your shape. On the **Swatches** tab:

- Click the ☐ **Fill** button and then click the scheme colour you want to apply to the shape's fill.

- Click the ☐ **Line** button and apply a different scheme colour to the shape's outline.

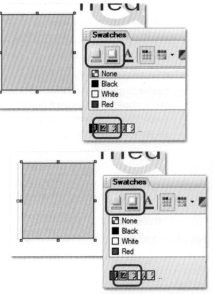

8 On the **Schemes** tab, click to apply a different colour scheme to the publication.

PagePlus applies the new scheme colours to the shape.

On the **Swatches** tab, notice that the colour scheme swatches have been replaced with the new scheme colours.

> ⓘ If you copy an object that uses scheme colours to another PagePlus document, the object will take on the colour scheme used in the new document.

As you can see, when you create new elements in a PagePlus document, or create a new publication from scratch, you can extend a colour scheme to your layout elements using the process just described.

You'll need to spend some time working out which colour combinations look best, but the mechanics of the process are simple.

Modifying colour schemes

If you've tried various colour schemes but haven't found one that's quite right for your document, you can modify any of the colours in an existing scheme to create a new one.

To modify a colour scheme

1 Right-click on the **Schemes** tab and select **Scheme Manager**.

On the **Edit** tab, the current scheme colours are displayed.

Each of the five scheme colour numbers (plus **Hyperlink**, **Followed Hyperlink**, and **Active Hyperlink** colours) has its own drop-down list, showing available colours in the PagePlus palette.

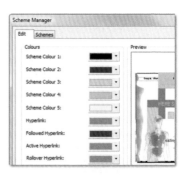

2 To set or change a scheme colour, simply click the button to expand the drop-down list, and then select a new colour.

3 **Optional step:** If the drop-down palette doesn't contain the colour you want to use, click **More Colours** to display the **Colour Selector**.

You can extend the **Colour Selector** dialog's publication palette using the **Palette Manager**, which lets you modify the current palette and also load and save named palettes.

For more information, see "Managing publication colours and palettes" in online Help.

In the **Colour Selector** dialog, various controls allow you to choose a colour to apply or mix your own custom colours.

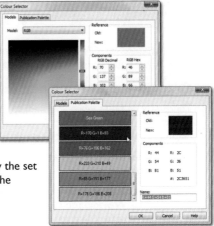

• The **Models** tab displays the colour space of the currently selected colour model.

• The **Publication Palette** tab lets you modify the set of colours associated with the current publication.

4　When you have modified your scheme on the **Edit** tab, save it by clicking **Save Scheme**.

The **Save Scheme** and **OK** buttons yield different results. Each PagePlus document stores a locally defined scheme, which may or may not correspond to a named scheme.

• Modifying a scheme in the **Scheme Manager** and then clicking **Save Scheme** updates the named scheme, but does not apply it to the publication.

• To ensure the publication uses the latest copy of the named scheme, click **OK** in the **Scheme Manager** or reapply the named scheme using the **Scheme Manager** or **Schemes** tab.

When modifying a scheme repeatedly, make sure your document is using the latest version.

5 In the **Save Scheme** dialog:

   • If you are modifying an existing scheme, leave the name unchanged and then click **OK**.

   • If you are creating a new scheme, type in a new name and then click **OK**.

6 If you have saved your changes with a new name, click the **Schemes** tab and then scroll the list to locate the new colour scheme.

Creating custom colour schemes from scratch

There may be times when you want to create a new colour scheme from scratch, perhaps using colours from your company logo or an image that features in your PagePlus document or on your Web site.

To complete the following section, you can use our sample photograph or any image of your choice.

You'll find the sample photograph, **Cocktail.jpg**, in the **...\Tutorials\Workspace\Colour Schemes** folder of your PagePlus installation directory. In a standard installation, this folder is copied to the following location:

C:\Program Files\Serif\PagePlus\X3

To create a custom colour scheme from an image

1 On the Tools toolbar, click 🖼 **Import Picture** and browse to locate the image you want to use.

2 Click **Open** and position the image on your page.

3 Select the image and then on the Picture context toolbar, click **Image Adjustments** (or right-click the image and choose **Image Adjustments**).

4 In the **Image Adjustments** dialog, click **Add Adjustment** and then select **Median**.

The **Median** adjustment panel, containing a **Radius** slider, is added to the dialog.

5 Drag the slider to the right so that colours making up the image blend into colour 'blocks,' as illustrated. Click **OK**.

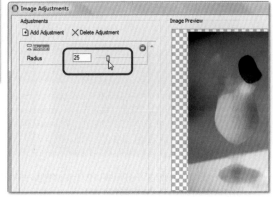

○ The **Median** filter is normally used to reduce 'noise' in an image.

6 Back in the PagePlus workspace, on the Tools toolbar, select the ▢ **Quick Rectangle** and draw a small square on your page (ours was about 1.5 cm x 1.5 cm).

7 Select the shape, hold down the **Ctrl** key, and then drag to the right to create a copy.

8 Repeat the previous step to create five identical squares.

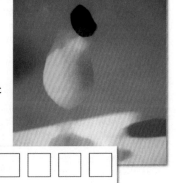

9 Select the first square, click the **Colour** tab, and then click the ✎ **Colour Picker**.

10 On the image, click and drag to select the first colour you want to add to your new colour scheme.

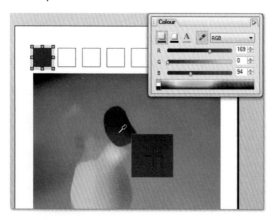

The popup colour sample updates as you drag to different areas of the image.

When you are happy with the colour displayed in the sample, release the mouse button.

The selected colour is applied to the square, and added to the ⊞ **Publication Palette** on the **Swatches** tab.

11 Selecting each of the remaining squares in turn, repeat the previous step to fill the shapes with four additional colours from your image.

12 On the **Swatches** tab, scroll to the end of the palette swatches to find your new custom colours displayed.

We're now ready to create our new colour scheme.

💡 You don't have to use QuickShapes to display your selected colours, but we think it's useful to see the colour swatches next to each other and the image on the page.

This allows you to determine if the colours work together with the image, and when isolated from the image. You can quickly and easily adjust the colours, pick new ones, or change the colour order, before deciding on your final scheme colours.

We used five squares—one for each main scheme colour—but you can create more than this to begin with. Once you've filled your squares with a selection of colours you can then decide on your final palette.

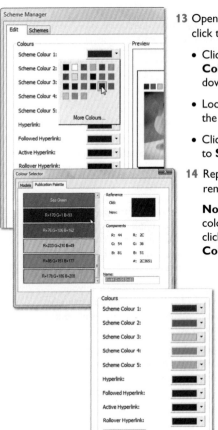

13 Open the **Scheme Manager** and click the **Edit** tab.

- Click the arrow next to **Scheme Colour 1** to expand the drop-down palette.

- Locate the colours you added in the previous steps.

- Click the colour you want to assign to **Scheme Colour 1**.

14 Repeat step 12 to assign the remaining scheme colours.

Note: If you don't see your colours in the drop-down palette, click **More Colours** to open the **Colour Selector** dialog.

On the **Publication Palette** tab, you will find the colours at the end of the palette list. Click the colour you want to assign to the scheme swatch, and then click **OK**.

15 Click **Save Scheme** and type a name for your colour scheme.

16 On the **Schemes** tab, scroll to find your new colour scheme.

17 Click the **Swatches** tab. Note that the swatches at the bottom of the tab now display your custom scheme colours.

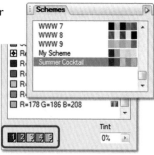

You can use these swatches to apply scheme colours to objects on your page.

Congratulations, you've created a custom colour scheme from scratch! It's a relatively simple process, but one which we hope you'll find useful in your future PagePlus publications.

Note that colour schemes are saved globally, so you'll be able to apply this scheme to your future PagePlus publications.

We'll conclude this tutorial with a brief discussion about colour in general. While the use of colour is quite personal, our aim is to help you choose colours that are not only visually pleasing but also reflect the content of your publication.

Choosing colours

Designers use many different methods to choose colours for their documents and Web sites. In the following example, we have based our colour scheme on an image that we want to use on the front cover of a brochure. As mentioned previously, you might also take colours from a company logo or some other 'signature' image.

Alternatively, you could use an image that does not appear in your document, but which contains a range of colours you find particularly attractive and which portrays the mood and message you want your publication, or Web site, to convey to your audience.

If you want a more structured approach, you can even employ a little basic colour theory! A quick Internet search will provide you with lots of information on this subject—try searching on "use of colour in print (or Web) design" for example.

In this section, we'll step you through the following approaches:

Example 1: Find an image or photograph that portrays the mood or message of the document or site—this may not necessarily be related to the content—then choose a range of colours from the image.

Example 2: Choose a 'base' colour (you can take this from an image that will feature in your publication), then use colour theory to find colours that harmonize with it.

> 🔔 Don't underestimate the importance of colour choice when designing your PagePlus document or Web site.
>
> No matter how professional your layout or how interesting your content, incorrect use of colour can result in pages that are ugly and/or difficult to read.

Example 1: Using an image or photograph

Suppose we're creating a brochure for a health spa. The first thing we need to do is think about the image we want to portray. We associate health spas with calmness and tranquility—it makes sense, therefore, not to use harsh or vibrant colours in our layouts.

1   Choose a few images that suit the mood. You could use a photograph, or an image found on the Internet or in a book or magazine (you'll need to scan the image so that you can open it on your computer).

The colour palettes of the following photographs all reflect the mood we want our brochure to convey.

Looking at these images, it's obvious that they fall into two distinct groups: one group contains various shades of blue along with natural and more muted tones; in the other group, softer earth tones predominate.

2   At this point, you (or your client) must decide which colour palette to use. For this tutorial, we'll assume that our health spa client prefers the muted tones of the 'pebbles' close-up photo.

3   You can now follow the procedure outlined previously to create your custom colour scheme (see "Creating custom colour schemes from scratch").

We suggest you start by creating lots of squares and fill them with a range of colours from the image.

When you have a good selection from which to choose, play around with the swatches and try different groupings before settling on your final five scheme colours.

4   If the choice is not obvious to you, create several different schemes using variations of your colour swatches. You can then switch between schemes to see how the look and feel of the publication changes.

Can't decide which colour palette to use? It's a good idea to create a PagePlus colour scheme for each palette, and then 'mock up' a page using each scheme.

You might also do this if you're designing a document for a client and want to present them with a few options from which to choose.

Example 2: Using colour theory

This method starts with the selection of a 'base' colour. You can choose any colour you prefer.

In our example, we'll take our base colour from a photograph that will feature on the front cover of a 'Kids' Camp' brochure

1   Follow the procedure outlined previously to extract a wide range of colours from your image (see "Creating custom colour schemes from scratch").

- Don't forget to add the **Median** image adjustment first, to create blocks of colour to work with.

- Start with the 'big' colours. These are the ones you see first when you glance at the image: skin, hair, and shirt. Then extract the 'small' colours—mouth, eyes, highlights and shadows.

- You need a good range of colours, but don't overdo it or you'll find it difficult to make your selection. You might only extract eight or ten colours, or you might find you need more. The exact number will vary depending on your image.

2 Group your results by colour, then sort each colour group by value from dark to light, deleting any colours that are too similar.

3 Select any one of your colours as your 'base.' Locate the colour on the colour wheel to determine whether it is warm or cool, and to see its relationship to other colours.

- Our **warm colours** are found in the red areas of girl's shirt, and in her hair and skin tones. Choose from these colours if your aim is to give a softer, gentler look and feel to your publication.

- Our **cool colours** are derived from the blue and white areas of the shirt, and from the eyes. These colours are generally used when a more serious or business-like approach is required.

4 Using your base colour and its position on the colour wheel, you can now start to create a range of colour palettes. There are several approaches you can take, including:

- Analogous

- Monochromatic

- Complement

- Split complement

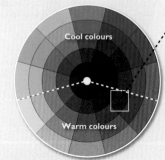

The Colour Wheel

The colour wheel is a basic model. It is meant as a guide only, so don't worry if you can't find an exact match for your colour.

Once you've located your base colour you can see its relationship to other colours and can then create a range of colour palettes that will work for your Web site.

Analogous colour palettes

Analogous colours are extracted from the two sections that sit either side of the base colour section.

These colours all share the same undertone—in our example, red-orange, red, and red-purple.

Analogous colour combinations are great for print or Web design as they are harmonious and very easy to work with.

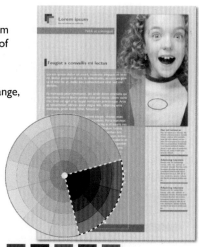

Monochromatic colour palettes

Monochromatic palettes consist of the dark, medium, and light values (the shades and tints) of your base colour.

You can choose your colour swatch values from the PagePlus palette, and then further increase the contrast by adjusting the **Tint** value on the **Swatches** tab.

- A shade is made by adding black to a colour to darken it.

- A tint is made by adding white to a colour to lighten it.

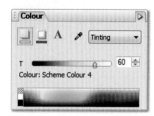

Complement colour palettes

You'll find the complement colours directly opposite the base colour range. Generally, the complement (in our case, the green range) is used as an accent.

These palettes provide extreme contrast, conveying energy and excitement. While often used in printed media, you should be wary of using this palette in Web design as such highly contrasted colours tend to be jarring to the eye when viewed on screen.

Split complement colour palettes

The split complement colours are the analogous colours of the complement itself.

Less jarring than the complement, this combination provides a more subtle contrast and a more harmonious palette.

In this example, the base colour red would be used as the accent colour in our design layout.

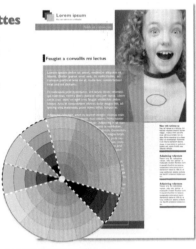

Mixing palettes

If you're feeling adventurous, you can also combine palettes to create some interesting effects.

For example, try contrasting your **base** colour and its **analogous** colours with the **complement**.

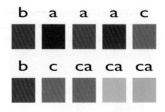

Alternatively, you could combine your **base** colour and its **complement** with the **complement's analogous** colours.

As you can see from our illustrations, each palette creates quite a different effect when applied to the same layout. Which one you choose depends on the message you want your publication to convey to your audience.

Accessibility

When choosing your colour schemes, it is worth bearing in mind that a small percentage of the population cannot differentiate between certain colours (the most common being red and green). To illustrate this, here are a few examples of the colour wheel when viewed by someone with one of the three main forms of colour blindness, protanope, deuteranope, and the rare tritanope:

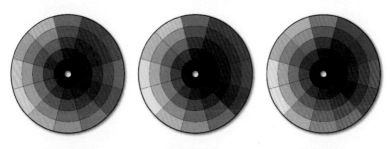

Protanope   Deuteranope   Tritanope

There is an excellent Web site called Vischeck that explains colour blindness in more detail. It also has a free plugin available for download that allows you to test your own site for colour use. The plugin works with Serif PhotoPlus and was used to create the images found within this tutorial.

Visit the site at http://www.vischeck.com/

The following sample image serves well to illustrate the care needed when deciding on colour schemes. This example simulates deuteranope colour blindness, the most common of the three types mentioned here. Notice how the browns and the reds appear almost identical.

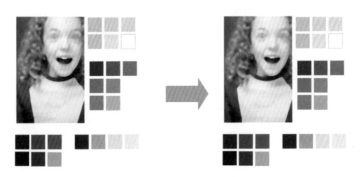

That concludes our tutorial. We've covered a lot of material here; we hope you've enjoyed working through the exercises and have learned something along the way. You should now be feeling comfortable creating your own colour schemes from scratch, and understand a little more about effective use of colour in design.

Have fun experimenting!

Design Packs

PagePlus Design Packs

PagePlus X3 provides a selection of **Design Pack** templates that you can use as starting points for your own publications.

Available from the **Program CD** and **Resource DVD**, these template sets provide a wide range of document types. The following categories may be included in each 'themed' pack:

- Brochures
- Business Cards
- Compliment Slips
- Emails
- Envelopes (C4, C5, DL)
- Flyers
- Letterheads
- Logos
- Menus
- Newsletters
- Posters
- Web Sites

To access the Design Packs:

1   From the **Startup Wizard**, select **Create > Use Design Template**.

2   In the **Choose a Template** dialog:

- Browse to and select the **Design Pack Template** you want to use.

- Click **Open**.

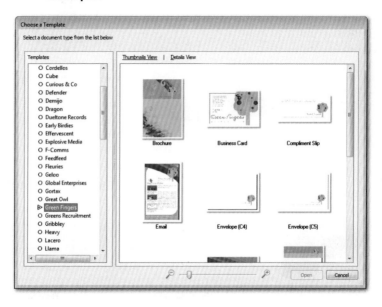

For more information about **Design Templates**, see "Creating a publication from a design template" in online Help.

The following pages provide previews of the **Design Pack** publications available on the **PagePlus X3 Program CD** and **Resource DVD**.

Logo

Front Cover

Inside Spread

Brochure

Back Cover

Letterhead

Newsletter

Envelopes (C4, C5, DL)

Business Card

Compliment Slip

Web Site

Email

Poster

Flyer

Logo

Newsletter

1 of 4

2 of 4

3 of 4

4 of 4

Posters

Web Site

Email

Logo

Front Cover

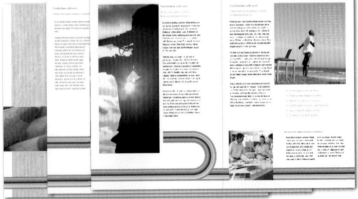

Inside Spread

Brochure

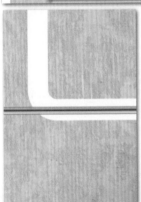

Back Cover

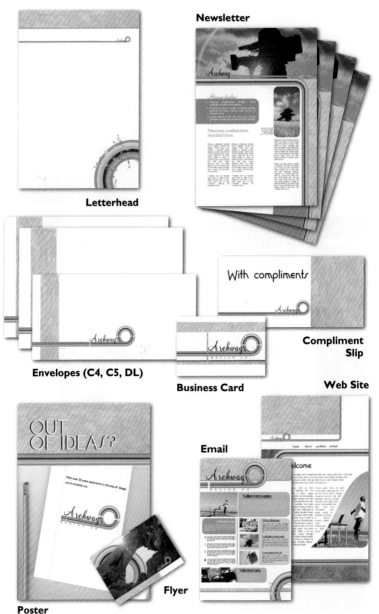

Letterhead

Newsletter

Envelopes (C4, C5, DL)

Business Card

Compliment Slip

Web Site

Email

Poster

Flyer

Logo

Front Cover

Inside Spread

Brochure

Back Cover

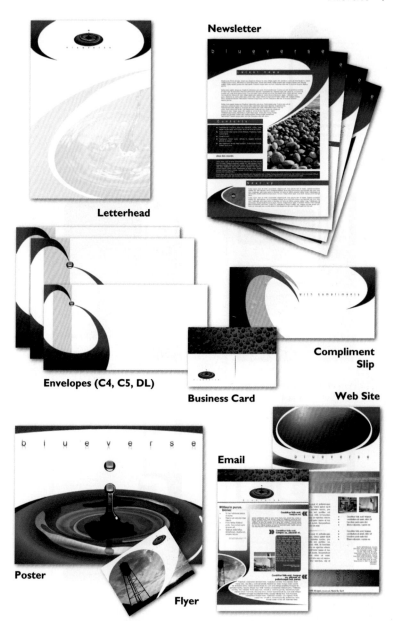

Letterhead

Newsletter

Envelopes (C4, C5, DL)

Business Card

Compliment Slip

Web Site

Poster

Email

Flyer

Logo

Newsletter

1 of 4

2 of 4

3 of 4

4 of 4

Poster

Web Site

Email

Logo

Front Cover

Inside Spread

Brochure

Back Cover

Newsletter

Letterhead

Envelopes (C4, C5, DL)

Compliment Slip

Business Card

Web Site

Email

Poster

Flyer

Logo

Menu

Front

Inside

Back

Inside Back

Compliment Slip

WITH COMPLIMENTS

cordellos

Letterhead

cordellos

Business Card

Poster

Logo

Front Cover

Inside Spread

Brochure

Back Cover

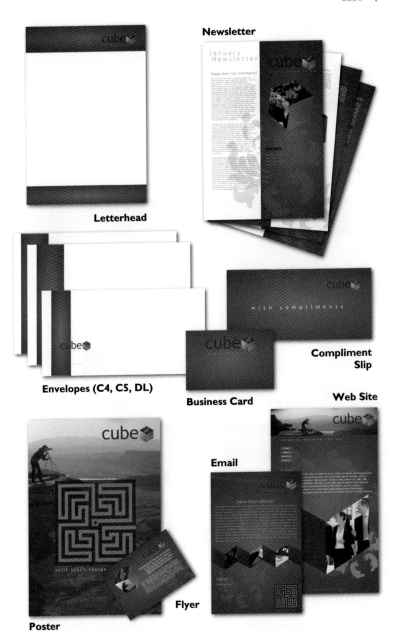

Letterhead

Newsletter

Envelopes (C4, C5, DL)

Business Card

Compliment Slip

Web Site

Email

Poster

Flyer

Logo

Newsletter

1 of 4

2 of 4

3 of 4

4 of 4

Poster

Web Site

Email

Logo

Front Cover

Inside Spread

Brochure

Back Cover

Letterhead

Newsletter

Envelopes (C4, C5, DL)

Compliment
Slip

Business Card

Web Site

Email

Poster

Flyer

Logo

Front Cover

Inside Spread

Brochure

Back Cover

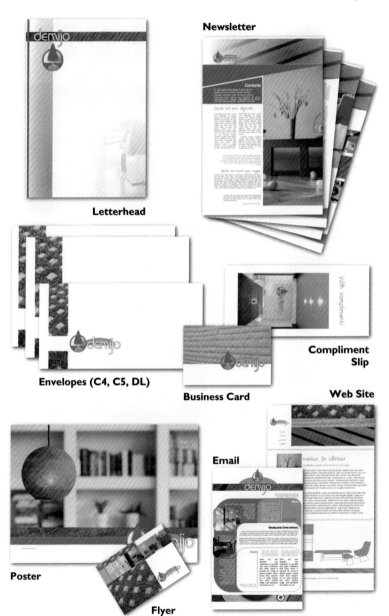

Newsletter

Letterhead

Envelopes (C4, C5, DL)

Business Card

Compliment
Slip

Web Site

Email

Poster

Flyer

Logo

Front Cover

Inside Spread

Brochure

Back Cover

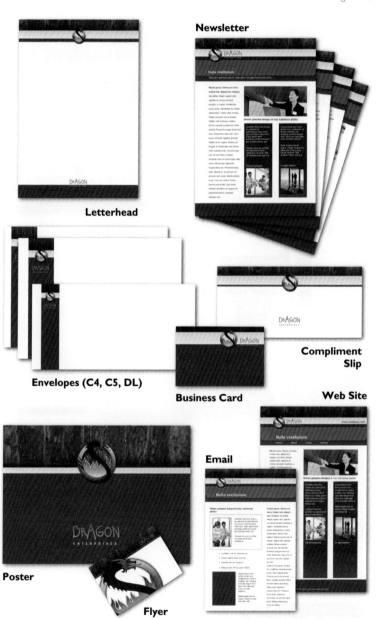

Newsletter

Letterhead

Envelopes (C4, C5, DL)

Business Card

Compliment Slip

Web Site

Email

Poster

Flyer

Logo

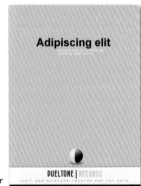

Front Cover

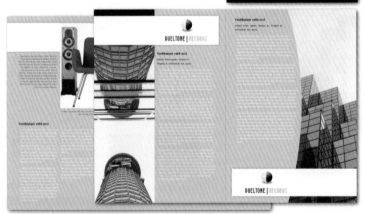

Inside Spread

Brochure

Back Cover

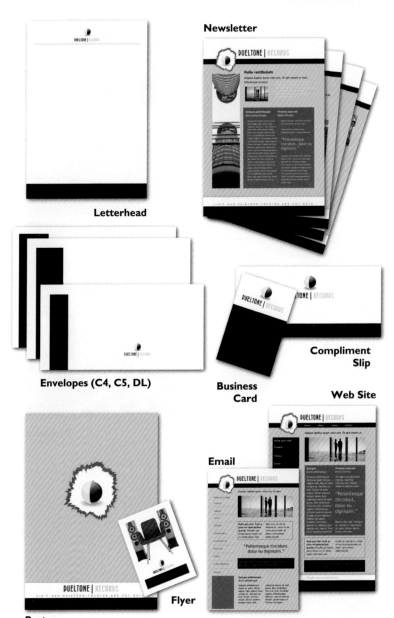

Newsletter

Letterhead

Envelopes (C4, C5, DL)

Business Card

Compliment Slip

Web Site

Email

Poster

Flyer

Logo

Front Cover

Inside Spread

Brochure

Back Cover

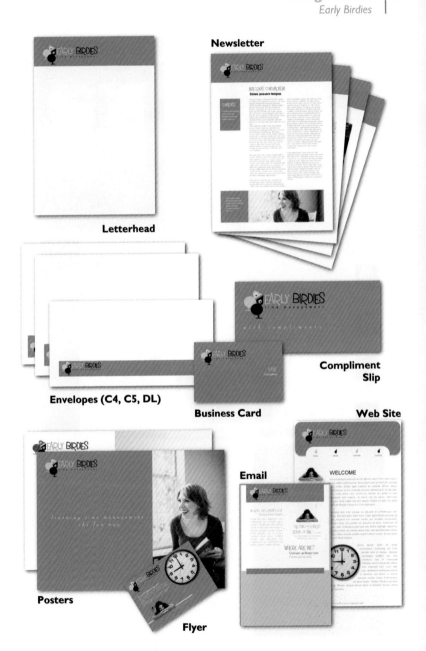

Newsletter

Letterhead

Envelopes (C4, C5, DL)

Business Card

Compliment Slip

Web Site

Email

Posters

Flyer

Logo

Front Cover

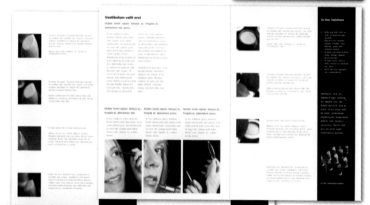

Inside Spread

Brochure

Back Cover

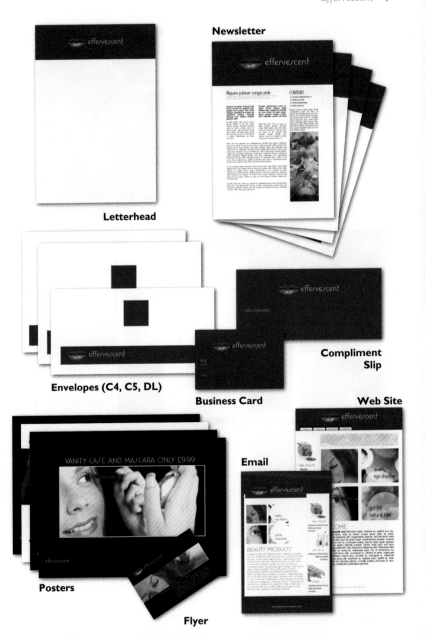

Newsletter

Letterhead

Envelopes (C4, C5, DL)

Business Card

Compliment Slip

Web Site

Email

Posters

Flyer

Logo

Front Cover

Inside Spread

Brochure

Back Cover

Letterhead

Newsletter

Envelopes (C4, C5, DL)

Compliment Slip

Business Card

Web Site

Poster

Flyer

Email

Logo

Front Cover

Inside Spread

Brochure

Back Cover

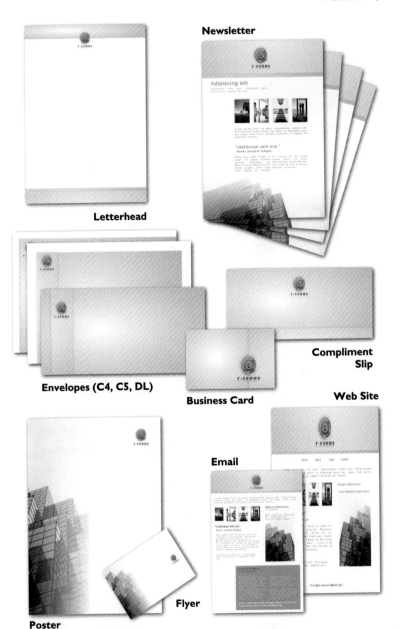

Newsletter

Letterhead

Compliment Slip

Envelopes (C4, C5, DL)

Business Card

Web Site

Email

Poster

Flyer

Logo

Menu

Front

Inside

Back

Inside Back

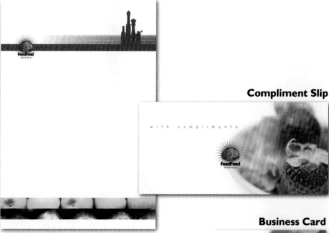

Compliment Slip

Business Card

Letterhead

Email

Poster

Logo

Front Cover

Inside Spread   **Brochure**

Back Cover

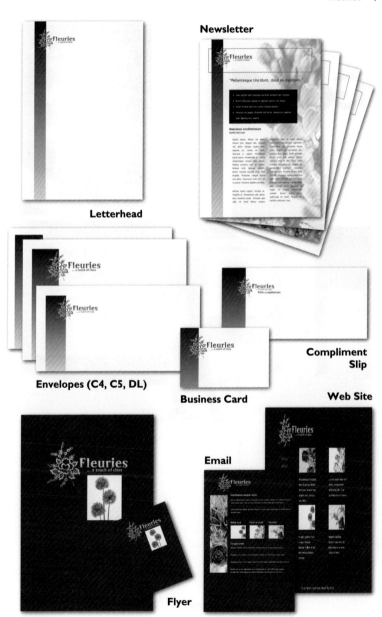

Newsletter

Letterhead

Envelopes (C4, C5, DL)

Business Card

Compliment Slip

Web Site

Poster

Email

Flyer

Logo

Front Cover

Inside Spread

Brochure

Back Cover

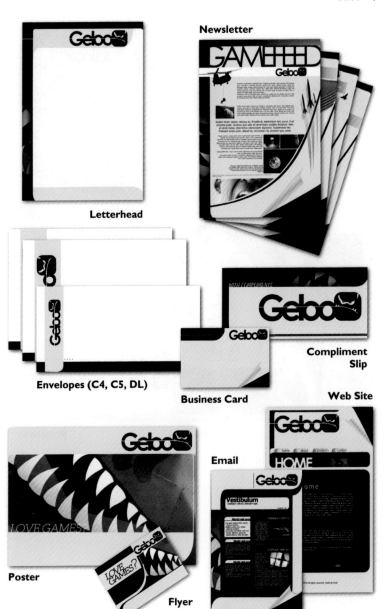

Newsletter

Letterhead

Envelopes (C4, C5, DL)

Business Card

Compliment Slip

Web Site

Email

Poster

Flyer

Logo

Front Cover

Inside Spread

Brochure

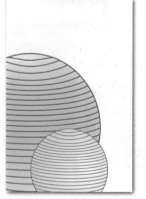

Back Cover

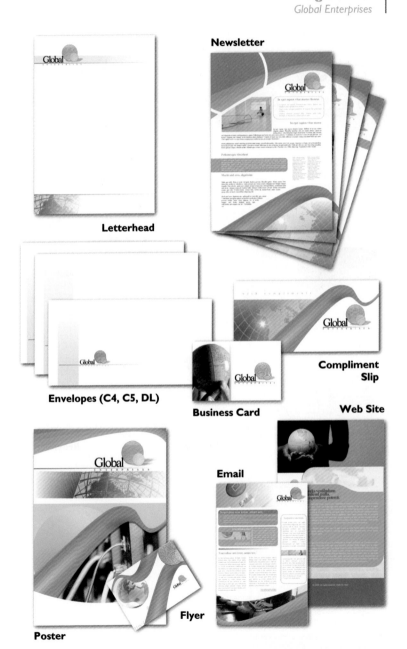

Letterhead

Newsletter

Envelopes (C4, C5, DL)

Business Card

Compliment Slip

Web Site

Email

Poster

Flyer

Logo

Front Cover

Inside Spread

Brochure

Back Cover

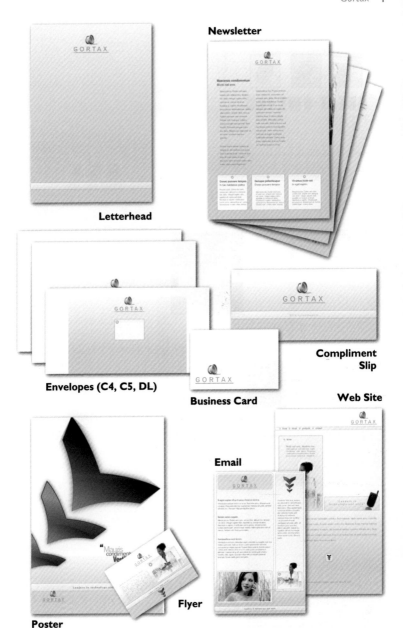

Newsletter

Letterhead

Envelopes (C4, C5, DL)

Compliment Slip

Business Card

Web Site

Email

Poster

Flyer

Logo

Front Cover

Inside Spread

Brochure

Back Cover

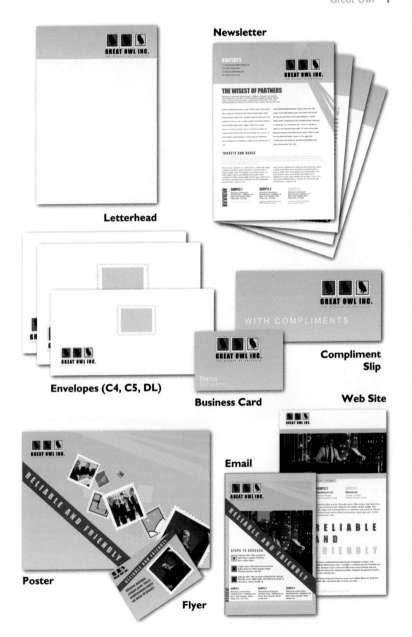

Newsletter

Letterhead

Envelopes (C4, C5, DL)

Business Card

Compliment Slip

Web Site

Email

Poster

Flyer

Logo

Front Cover

Inside Spread

Brochure

Back Cover

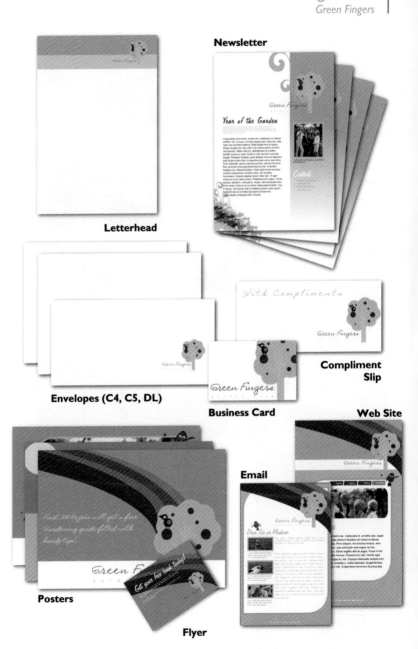

Newsletter

Letterhead

Compliment Slip

Envelopes (C4, C5, DL)

Business Card

Web Site

Email

Posters

Flyer

Logo

Front Cover

Inside Spread

Brochure

Back Cover

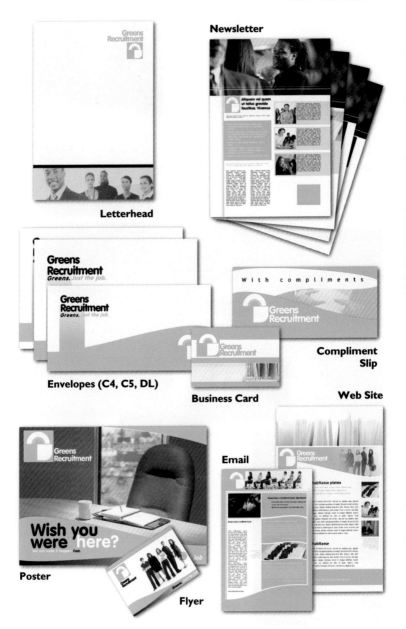

Newsletter

Letterhead

Envelopes (C4, C5, DL)

Business Card

Compliment Slip

Web Site

Email

Poster

Flyer

Logo

Front Cover

Inside Spread

Brochure

Back Cover

Newsletter

Letterhead

Envelopes (C4, C5, DL)

Compliment Slip

Business Card

Web Site

Email

Poster

Flyer

Logo

Front Cover

Inside Spread

Brochure

Back Cover

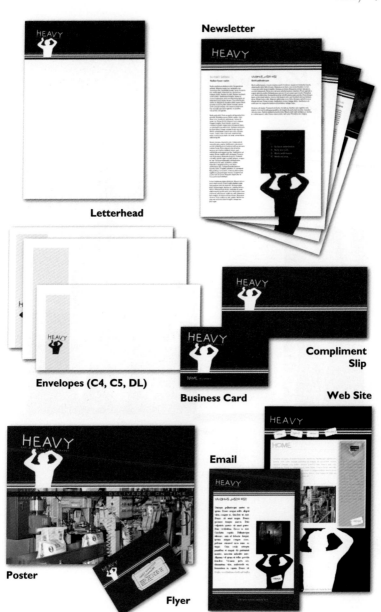

Newsletter

Letterhead

Envelopes (C4, C5, DL)

Business Card

Compliment Slip

Web Site

Email

Poster

Flyer

Logo

Front Cover

Inside Spread

Brochure

Back Cover

Newsletter

Letterhead

Compliment Slip

Envelopes (C4, C5, DL)

Business Card

Web Site

Email

Poster

Flyer

Logo

Front

Inside

Back

Inside Back

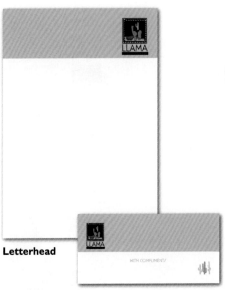

Letterhead

Email

Compliment Slip

Posters

Logo

Front Cover

Inside Spread

Brochure

Back Cover

Letterhead

Newsletter

Envelopes (C4, C5, DL)

Compliment Slip

Business Card

Web Site

Poster

Email

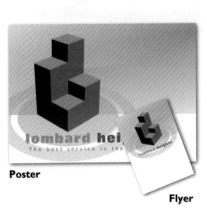

Flyer

Logo

Front Cover

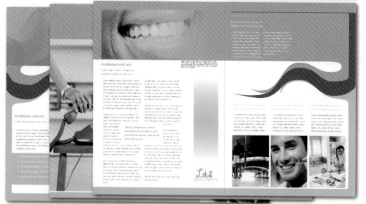

Inside Spread

Brochure

Back Cover

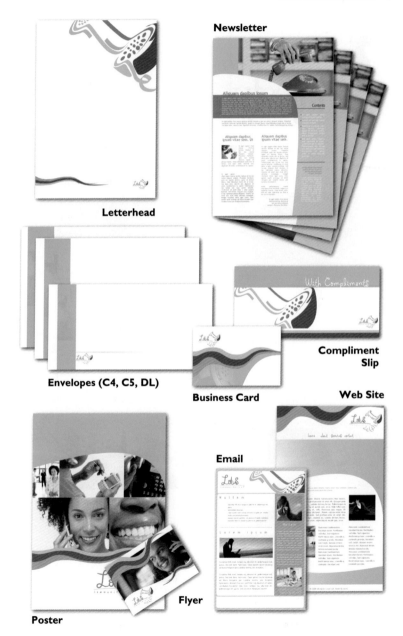

Newsletter

Letterhead

Envelopes (C4, C5, DL)

Business Card

Compliment Slip

Web Site

Email

Poster

Flyer

Logo

Newsletter

1 of 4

2 of 4

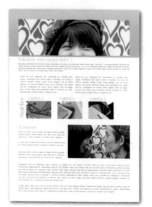

3 of 4

4 of 4

Poster

Web Site

Email

Logo

Front Cover

Inside Spread

Brochure

Back Cover

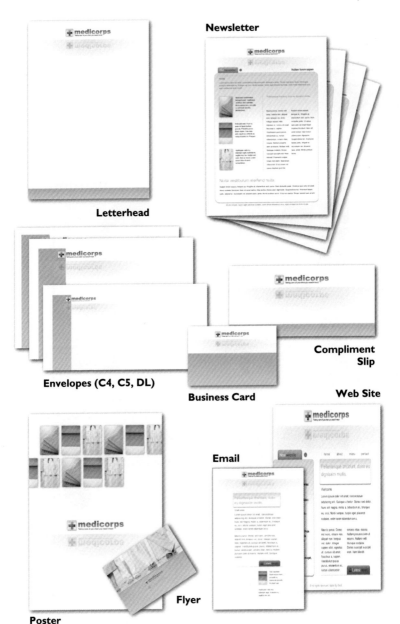

Letterhead

Newsletter

Envelopes (C4, C5, DL)

Compliment Slip

Business Card

Web Site

Email

Poster

Flyer

Logo

Newsletter

1 of 4

2 of 4

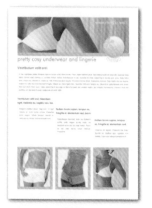

3 of 4

4 of 4

Poster

Web Site

Email

Logo

Front Cover

Inside Spread

Brochure

Back Cover

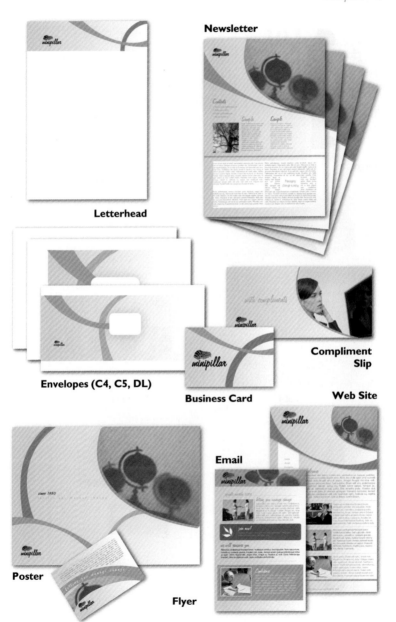

Newsletter

Letterhead

Envelopes (C4, C5, DL)

Business Card

Compliment Slip

Web Site

Email

Poster

Flyer

Logo

Newsletter

I of 4

2 of 4

3 of 4

4 of 4

Posters

Web Site

Email

Logo

Menu

Front

Inside

Back

Inside Back

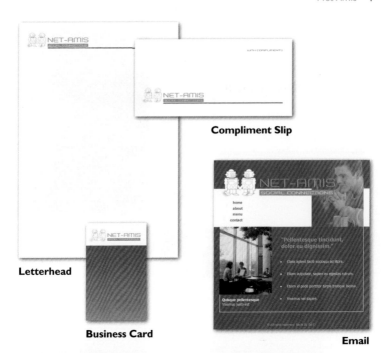

Compliment Slip

Letterhead

Business Card

Email

Poster

Logo

Front Cover

Inside Spread

Brochure

Back Cover

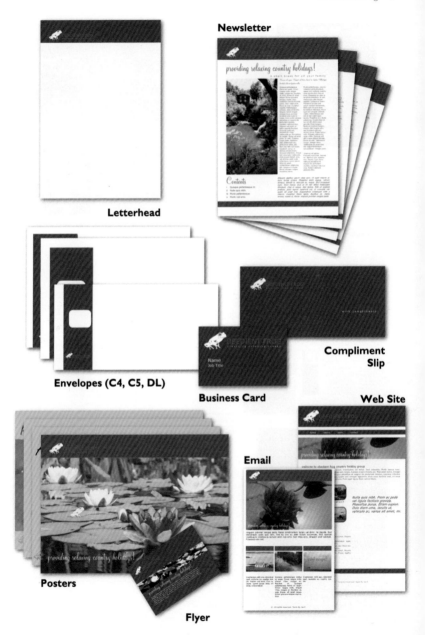

Newsletter

Letterhead

Envelopes (C4, C5, DL)

Business Card

Compliment Slip

Web Site

Email

Posters

Flyer

Logo

Front Cover

Inside Spread

Brochure

Back Cover

Letterhead

Newsletter

Envelopes (C4, C5, DL)

Business Card

Compliment Slip

Web Site

Email

Poster

Flyer

Logo

Front Cover

Inside Spread

Brochure

Back Cover

Newsletter

Letterhead

Envelopes (C4, C5, DL)

Compliment Slip

Business Card

Web Site

Email

Poster

Flyer

Logo

Front Cover

Inside Spread

Brochure

Back Cover

Newsletter

Letterhead

Envelopes (C4, C5, DL)

Business Card

Compliment Slip

Web Site

Email

Posters

Flyer

Logo

Newsletter

1 of 4

2 of 4

3 of 4

4 of 4

Posters

Web Site

Email

Logo

Newsletter

1 of 4

2 of 4

3 of 4

4 of 4

Poster

Web Site

Email

Logo

Front Cover

Inside Spread

Brochure

Back Cover

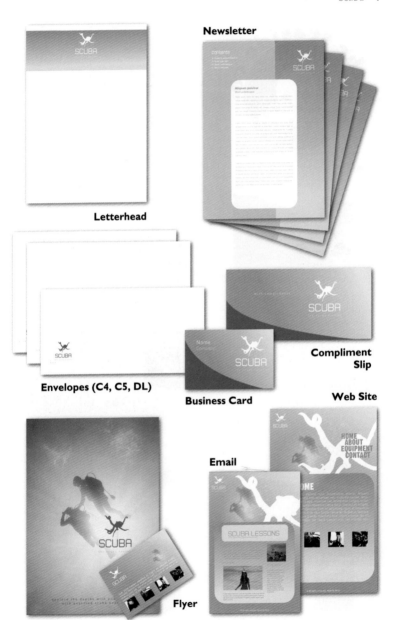

Newsletter

Letterhead

Envelopes (C4, C5, DL)

Business Card

Compliment Slip

Web Site

Email

Poster

Flyer

Logo

Newsletter

1 of 4

2 of 4

3 of 4

4 of 4

Posters

Web Site

Email

Logo

Newsletter

1 of 4

2 of 4

3 of 4

4 of 4

Poster

Web Site

Email

Logo

Front Cover

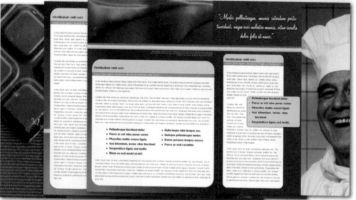

Inside Spread

Brochure

Back Cover

Newsletter

Letterhead

Envelopes (C4, C5, DL)

Business Card

With compliments

Compliment Slip

Web Site

Email

WE L♥VE chocolate

Poster

Flyer

Logo

Front Cover

Inside Spread

Brochure

Back Cover

Letterhead

Newsletter

Envelopes (C4, C5, DL)

Business Card

Compliment Slip

Web Site

Email

Poster

Flyer

Logo

Front Cover

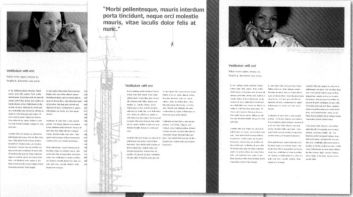

Inside Spread

Brochure

Back Cover

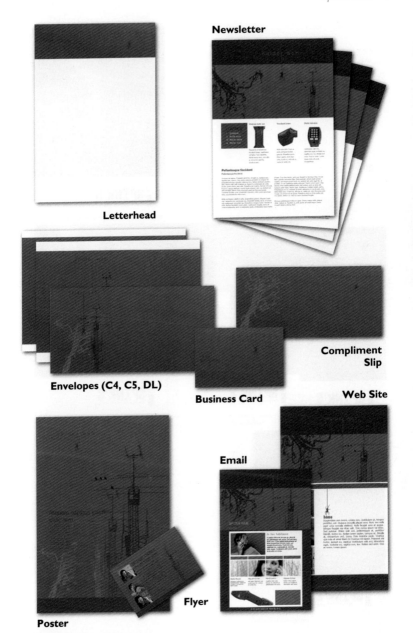

Newsletter

Letterhead

Envelopes (C4, C5, DL)

Business Card

Compliment Slip

Web Site

Email

Poster

Flyer

Logo

Front Cover

Inside Spread

Brochure

Back Cover

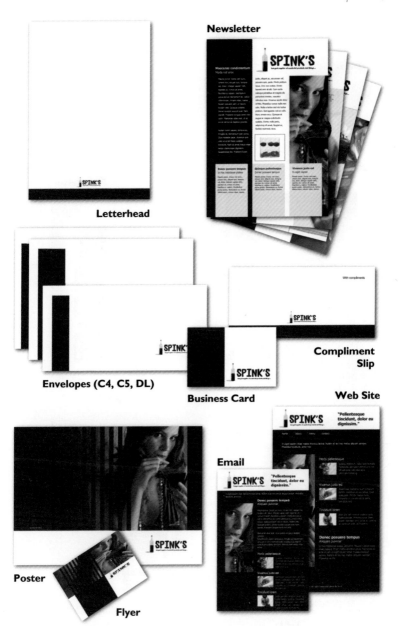

Newsletter

Letterhead

Compliment Slip

Envelopes (C4, C5, DL)

Business Card

Web Site

Email

Poster

Flyer

Logo

Newsletter

1 of 4

2 of 4

3 of 4

4 of 4

Poster

Web Site

Email

Logo

Front Cover

Inside Spread

Brochure

Back Cover

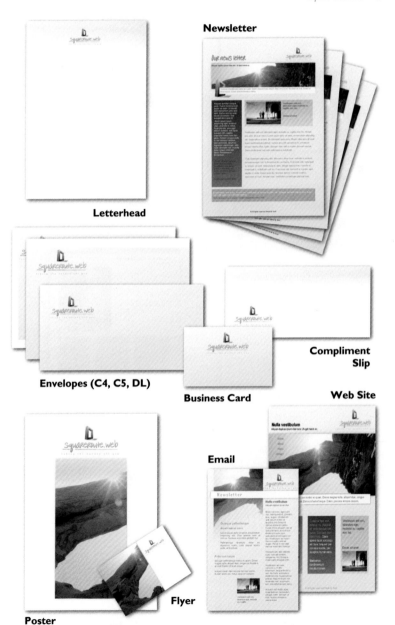

Newsletter

Letterhead

Envelopes (C4, C5, DL)

Business Card

Compliment Slip

Web Site

Email

Poster

Flyer

Logo

Newsletter

1 of 4

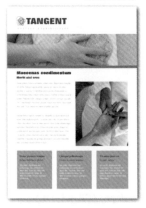

2 of 4

3 of 4

4 of 4

Poster

Web Site

Email

Logo

Front Cover

Inside Spread

Brochure

Back Cover

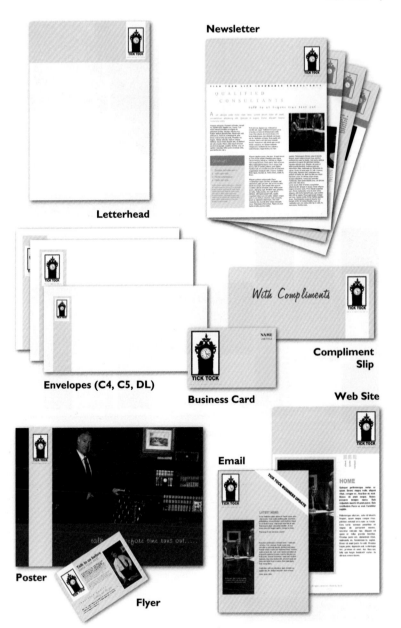

Newsletter

Letterhead

Envelopes (C4, C5, DL)

Business Card

With Compliments

Compliment Slip

Web Site

Email

Poster

Flyer

Logo

Front Cover

Inside Spread

Brochure

Back Cover

Newsletter

Letterhead

Envelopes (C4, C5, DL)

Business Card

Compliment Slip

Web Site

Email

Poster

Flyer

Logo

Front Cover

Inside Spread

Brochure

Back Cover

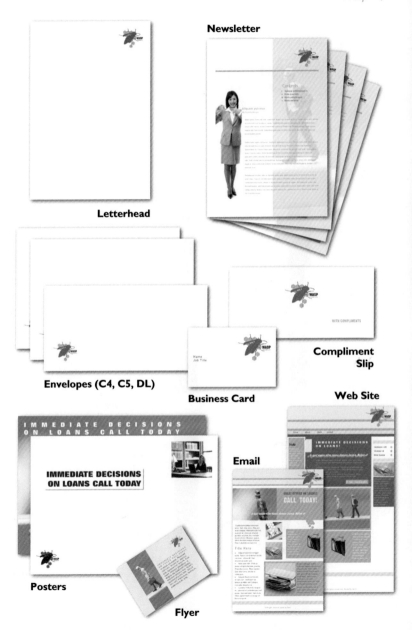

Newsletter

Letterhead

Envelopes (C4, C5, DL)

Business Card

Compliment Slip

Web Site

Posters

Email

Flyer

Logo

Menu

Front

Inside

Back

Inside Back

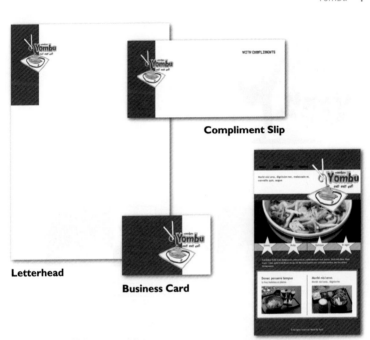

Compliment Slip

Letterhead

Business Card

Email

Poster

Logo

Newsletter

1 of 4

2 of 4

3 of 4

4 of 4

Poster

Web Site

Email

Logo

Front Cover

Inside Spread

Brochure

Back Cover

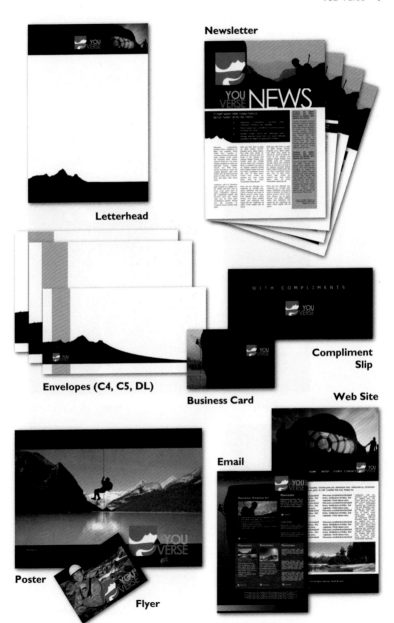

Newsletter

Letterhead

Envelopes (C4, C5, DL)

Business Card

Compliment Slip

Web Site

Email

Poster

Flyer

Logo

Menu

Front

Inside

Back

Inside Back

Compliment Slip

Letterhead

Business Card

Poster

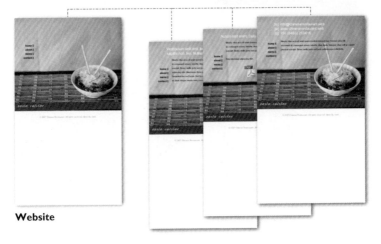

Website

LogoStudio & Logo Templates

LogoStudio

LogoStudio is a purpose-built environment that lets you create and edit logos in isolation from other page elements. You can create your own logos from scratch, or choose from a range of logo templates.

Transfer of data between LogoStudio and PagePlus is transparent and seamless, and you can jump between the two environments at any time.

Template Logos

The **PagePlus X3 Program CD** provides a wide selection of logo templates, each offering a choice of layouts and colour sets. You can use the templates 'as is,' or customize them to suit your needs.

The **Insert Logo** dialog also includes a collection of ready-made design elements (**Flashes**), which you can add to any of your publications.

> 🛈 A collection of **Sample Logos** is also available from the **Insert Logo** dialog, upon installation of the **PagePlus X3 Resource DVD**.

Using LogoStudio

LogoStudio's intuitive user interface focuses on the main tools and techniques you'll need, and provides step-by-step instructions to help you create and refine your logo.

To create a logo from scratch:

1 On the Tools toolbar, click 👁 **Insert Logo**.

2 In the **Insert Logo** dialog, select the blank thumbnail from the Blank section in the left pane.

3 Click **Open**.

4 Click or click and drag to place the logo on the page. The LogoStudio environment opens automatically.

5 To create your design, you can use the interactive **How To** tab elements, or the traditional PagePlus creation tools.

To edit an existing logo:

1 Click the 👁 **Edit in LogoStudio** button that displays on the control bar under the selected logo.

   - or -

   On the Tools toolbar, on the Logo flyout, click 👁 **Edit in LogoStudio**.

   - or -

   Right-click the logo and select **Edit in LogoStudio...**

   LogoStudio opens with your object(s) zoomed in to fit your workspace.

2 To customize your logo design, use the interactive **How To** tab elements, or the traditional PagePlus creation tools.

3 To exit LogoStudio and return to PagePlus, click ✕ Close LogoStudio on the LogoStudio main toolbar.

   The modified logo is updated in its original position.

> 💡 For more information on creating logos in LogoStudio, see the LogoStudio **How To** tab and *"Creating Logos"* in online Help.

To create a logo from an existing template:

1 On the Tools toolbar, click 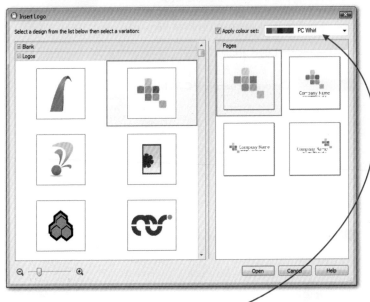 **Insert Logo**.

2 In the **Insert Logo** dialog, select a design template from the left pane, and then choose your template layout from the right pane. (These differ depending on the template chosen.)

3 In the upper right corner of the dialog:

- To apply the colour scheme of the publication, clear the **Use Colour Set** check box.

   - or -

- To apply a colour set, select the **Use Colour Set** check box, and then select a colour set from the drop-down list.

4 Click **Open**.

5 **Optional:** If you have chosen a logo containing text objects, the **Customize Your Logo** dialog opens, allowing you to edit the text.

6 Click **OK**.

7 To insert the logo at default size, click on your page; to set the size of the logo, click and drag out a region and release the mouse button.

Each **Logo Template** provides a choice of layouts and colour sets. In the example on the right, there are nine layout options (displayed below), including three colour set options.

The following pages display all of the logo templates. However, to get a real sense of their versatility, we suggest you browse the various layouts and colour sets for yourself, from the **Insert Logo** dialog.

Colour Scheme: PC Whirl

Company Name

Company Name

Company Name

Colour Scheme: Lab

Company Name

Company Name

Company Name

Colour Scheme: dot.com

Company Name

Company Name

Company Name